D0885195

Mary, Mother of Martyrs

HOW MOTHERHOOD BECAME SELF-SACRIFICE IN
EARLY CHRISTIANITY

Kathleen Gallagher Elkins

Feminist Studies in Religion
BOOKS

2018

Mary, Mother of Martyrs: How Motherhood Became Self-Sacrifice in Early Christianity

Image Copyright Information
Water of Life (detail) by Pacita Abad
Courtesy of Pacita Abad Art Real Estate

First published by Dog Ear Publishing
4011 Vincennes Road
Indianapolis, IN 46268
www.dogearpublishing.net

 Feminist Studies in Religion
BOOKS

ISBN: 978-1-4575-6237-2

This book is printed on acid free paper.
Printed in the United States of America

For Noah, who made me a mother

And for Derek, who reminds me not to be a martyr

Feminist Studies in Religion Books

Current titles
Congress of Wo/men: Religion, Gender, and Kyriarchal Power
By Elisabeth Schüssler Fiorenza

Sexual Violence and Sacred Texts
Edited by Amy Kalmanofsky

Women Religion Revolution
Edited by Xochitl Alvizo and Gina Messina

Contents

Acknowledgments

B ecause this book has its roots in my doctoral dissertation, it seems like an impossible task to thank all of the people who have helped along the way. At Drew University, I had the encouragement and wisdom of wonderful advisors and teachers: Melanie Johnson-DeBaufre, Virginia Burrus, and Stephen D. Moore comprised the extraordinary committee that pushed me to keep thinking and keep writing. I also had the good fortune to learn from Danna Nolan Fewell, Kenneth Ngwa, Althea Spencer-Miller, Kate Ott, and Traci West. Ernie Rubinstein, Kathy Juliano, Jody Caldwell, and Andrew Scrimgeour made the Drew Library a wonderful place to write. I'm lucky enough to call other NT/EC Drewids my dear friends; Shanell T. Smith, Christy Cobb, and Minta Fox are wise and delightful in equal measure. Jennifer Kaalund and Peter Mena made for the best writing group. Their insights, corrections, and critical questions are woven throughout this book. I am grateful to know all of you.

The community at St. Norbert College has supported me in many ways, including the editing of this book. The members of the Theology and Religious Studies discipline (Tom Bolin, Mara Brecht, Bridget Burke Ravizza, Howard Ebert, Reg Kim, Karen Park, Gerardo Rodriguez, and Paul Wadell) are inspiring colleagues and wonderful friends. Our teaching assistant Lauren March caught many mistakes and faithfully hunted down lost library books; she also created the indices. The "nasty women" in my faculty cohort (Raquel Cowell, Anna Herrman, and Abby Trollinger—and Ivy Cargile, too, even though you left the frozen tundra) are some of my favorite humans on the planet. I still find myself surprised at my good fortune in landing at St. Norbert and in calling each of you friends.

MARY, MOTHER OF MARTYRS

The editors of FSR Books and other folks associated with Feminist Studies in Religion, Inc., have been delightful to work with. Many thanks to Melanie Johnson-DeBaufre, Kate Ott, Elisabeth Schüssler Fiorenza, Stephanie May, Shelly Matthews, Heather Lee Miller, and especially Nikki Hoskins, who has cheerfully put up with so many last-minute emails from me.

While writing and researching about ancient families, I was often conscious of the ways that my own family has supported my academic work. I am grateful to my parents (whether by blood or by marriage): Kevin and Kathleen Gallagher, Nancy Kriegner, and Jerry and Lisa Elkins. My siblings are witty, brilliant, and a joy to be around: Kevin, Colleen, and Johnny Gallagher, Wade Elkins, and Steven Strafford. My extended families have often asked after the progress of the book and generally made me feel that I had something important to say; my aunts Ann Denvir and Joyce Gallagher deserve special mention here. I love all of you very much.

Two people who were significant sources of support died during the time I was editing this work: my uncle Quin Denvir and my undergraduate mentor, Barnes Tatum. Though they didn't know each other, I think they would have gotten along well; both had quirky senses of humor and brilliant minds and were committed to doing good in the world. I think they would have been proud of me, and I wish they could see the finished book.

Last, and most important, Derek and Noah are the ones nearest to my heart—and to my own mothering. I am grateful to them both for more things than I can name, especially the ways in which they make our home a place of love, warmth, and laughter. I'm consistently amazed and delighted by both of them. They also helpfully remind me to put down the books and come throw the football, and so I dedicate this book to them. Now, let's go play.

Kathleen Gallagher Elkins
March 25, 2017
(Feast of the Annunciation)

Introduction

A student gave me a Christmas card last year; on the front is an image of Eve and Mary. Eve's eyes are downcast, she's covered by her hair, and she is holding an apple in one hand and Mary's hand in the other. Mary is chastely dressed, heavily pregnant, and holding Eve's cheek with her free hand. Along the bottom of the image is a serpent; its body is coiled around Eve's feet, nearly tripping her, while its head is being crushed under Mary's foot. The poem on the inside reads:

> My mother, my daughter, Life-giving, Eve
> Do not be ashamed, do not grieve
> The former things have passed away,
> Our God has brought us to a New Day.
> See, I am with Child,
> Through whom all will be reconciled.
> O Eve! My sister, my friend,
> We will rejoice together
> Forever
> Life without end.[1]

The image and poem evoke a range of issues related to Mary, Eve, women's roles, and redemption. What is perhaps hidden in this peaceful image is the role of suffering: Eve mourns and the snake threatens, but Mary shows no worry or pain. Knowing the Christmas story, we might expect some fear on the holy mother's face. Although other iconic images of Mary, such as the *Pietà* and "Stabat Mater," are

---

[1] The image and poem text are available at http://www.monasterycandy.com; the sisters of Our Lady of the Mississippi Abbey in Dubuque, Iowa, sell the card. The drawing is by Sr. Grace Remington, OSCO. Thanks to Hannah for the card.

bound up with ideas about suffering, sacrifice, and loss, here, she is passive, peaceful, and accepting.

The figure of Mary, whether she is depicted as serene or threatened, is persistently connected to notions about self-sacrifice. She is idealized in Christian traditions as the paradigmatic self-sacrificing mother who willingly accepts an unexpected pregnancy and passively accepts her son's violent death. No wonder mothers are expected to naturally, normally, and unreservedly sacrifice everything for their children! Mary is often held up as the ideal mother to whom all women (mothers or not) must aspire. Feminist theologians have questioned the ways in which Mary is idealized: How can any woman hope to be both virgin and mother? Why should women serenely accept an unexpected pregnancy? How could mothers welcome the deaths of their children?

Mary is not the only self-sacrificing mother in the Bible; indeed, other maternal figures whose narratives involve self-sacrifice and martyrdom appear in both canonical and noncanonical texts. If we consider Mary alongside other mothers who sacrifice, something new emerges: We see a diversity of images related to maternity, sacrifice, and loss. Moreover, highlighting the complex linkages among these narratives gives a kaleidoscopic image; one slight turn of the cylinder shows that the issues being raised in each narrative are varied. Ancient authors (and modern interpreters, although differently) used these maternal figures to reflect on sacrifice and motherhood, of course, but also on communal identity formation, transformative pain, the role of violence, and the development of traditions.

In what follows, I consider four textual sites where mothering is presented or discussed as intimately connected to self-sacrifice. First, I discuss Mary the mother of Jesus, focusing primarily (but not exclusively) on infancy and crucifixion stories (especially Matt. 1:18–2:23, Luke 1–2, and John 19:25–27). Scholars often highlight those texts when discussing Mary as an idealized, self-sacrificing mother, creating and evaluating a composite image of Mary across the gospels. Examining the way the figure of Mary is different in each gospel context resists the tendency to essentialize (early) Christian motherhood and self-sacrifice. Next, I turn to the Woman

Clothed with the Sun (Rev. 12:1–17), who labors and births a son while a great dragon threatens to devour her child. The Book of Revelation includes a few other endangered mothers; both "that woman Jezebel" (2:20–23) and "Babylon the great" (17:1–18:24) have symbolic children and face violence that is sanctioned by heavenly beings. I consider the ways in which these texts in the Book of Revelation present motherhood as both a threatened and threatening subjectivity, while also examining the various ways that scholars read these rival maternal figures. Then I examine the Maccabean mother with seven sons (4 Macc. 8–18), who encourages her children to remain steadfast to their ancestral customs, even though it will result in their deaths. I examine how this text and its interpreters deliberate on ideal motherly bonds with children in relation to the competing demands of ethnoreligious and national solidarity. Moreover, I discuss the complex boundary-making that is accomplished in and through these different texts. Last, I consider the two eponymous mother-martyrs who give up their children in the *Passion of Perpetua and Felicitas*. This narrative provides scholars a place from which to discuss the complex relationship between motherhood and agency, as well as the ways in which the production of Christian identity intersects with status, the family, and ethnicity. Considering these texts together recognizes that both canonical and noncanonical texts (and texts later classified as "Jewish" or "Christian") have been part of the formation of the Christian tradition and are sites for entering modern scholarly debates about feminism, women's roles, and sacrifice.

Although I consider all of these maternal figures as as examples of self-sacrifice, I recognize that the modes of sacrificing are varied. The Maccabean mother, Perpetua, and Felicitas all accept violent death at the hands of persecutors, whereas Mary watches her son suffer an excruciating death at the hands of the state. She herself does not die a violent death as the other figures do, yet Mary is often associated with self-denial and loss (as demonstrated in images such as the *Pietà* or in her title Mother of Sorrows), and the Annunciation scene especially seems to represent a moment of self-sacrifice on her part, as she displays willingness to parent an unexpected child.

Though the deaths of the maternal figures in Revelation are not narrated, these figures are threatened with death or punishment. They stand in contrast to the bride, Jerusalem, whom Revelation presents as inviolable and unharmed. Considering all of these texts together shows the diverse forms that self-sacrifice can take (for example, sacrifice on behalf of one's child or children, sacrifice of one's own life, or sacrifice of one's children).

The figure of the mother—especially a suffering, self-sacrificing mother—does diverse kinds of rhetorical work and is produced for various reasons in both ancient texts and modern debates. Enduring transformative pain (perhaps paralleling the pain of childbirth, which is transformed into joy at the birth of a child) is a common trope in these texts; Perpetua and Felicitas first accept separation from their children (indeed, Felicitas prays for labor to begin prematurely so she can enter the arena with her co-martyrs), prefiguring their acceptance of painful deaths. Likewise, the Maccabean mother encourages her children to accept their own deaths, even though this is against her maternal nature (4 Macc. 14:13–20) and causes her to suffer the "instruments of torture employed against each one of the children" (14:12). In Revelation, the narrator focuses on the Sun Woman's birth pangs (12:2) while a dragon lurks nearby, waiting to devour her newborn son. As mother of a crucified messianic figure and as a classic model of traditional femininity, Mary submits to God and endures the violent fate of her son. Maternal suffering pulls at audiences' heartstrings; thus, self-sacrificing mothers are powerfully useful and flexible figures for reflecting on the fecund transformations of pain and suffering, yet the results of such depictions are complex. Potentially problematic and potentially powerful, the image of the early Christian self-sacrificing mother performs complex women's work.

Approaching Maternal Self-Sacrifice as a Flexible Discourse

Elisabeth Schüssler Fiorenza has been a persistent voice in the field of biblical studies for investigating the stated and unstated politics of interpretation. Notably, she has called for biblical scholars to assess whether interpretive practices "do justice not only to the text and its interpretations but also to contemporary readers, especially to those biblical readers who are affected by biblical texts today."[2] Likewise, Elizabeth Castelli and Hal Taussig, in their consideration of Christian origins and historiography, acknowledge that

> most people who work on Christian origins are working on texts that have shaped contemporary social relations and political expectations in the West, texts that are routinely trotted out to support or oppose one political or social practice or another. Indeed, reference to the Bible as a "natural" source of authority for underwriting a wide variety of social and political claims continues apace, largely unchallenged and uninterrogated (least of all by scholars who have dedicated their professional careers to the study of the texts and their ancient contexts).[3]

Inspired by the call of Schüssler Fiorenza and of Castelli and Taussig, I employ feminist rhetorical analysis to attend to both the rhetoricity of the ancient texts and the politics of interpretation in the scholarly analyses of these maternal figures.

Scholarship on families, agency, and sacrifice in antiquity often engages and concerns itself with modern political claims about "family values" and with pop-Freudian ideas about the crucial role of the mother in a young child's life, though that interestedness is sometimes concealed or unrecognized. Scholars sometimes claim to be making better historical arguments, rather than acknowledge that academics, through teaching and scholarship, engage and contribute to discussions in the public square.[4] This book thus attempts to practice "criti-

---

[2] Elisabeth Schüssler Fiorenza, *Rhetoric and Ethic: The Politics of Biblical Studies* (Minneapolis, MN: Fortress, 1999), 197.

[3] Elizabeth A. Castelli and Hal Taussig, "Drawing Large and Startling Figures: Reimagining Christian Origins by Painting Like Picasso," in *Reimagining Christian Origins: A Colloquium Honoring Burton L. Mack*, ed. Elizabeth A. Castelli and Hal Taussig (Valley Forge, PA: Trinity Press International, 1996), 16.

[4] Elisabeth Schüssler Fiorenza, "Reading Scripture in the Context of Empire," in *The Bible in the Public Square: Reading the Signs of the Times*, ed. Cynthia Briggs Kittredge,

cal reflexivity"—that is, to investigate not only what we read but also how we read, "analyzing how our readings shape and are shaped by our current contexts."[5] In a cultural context that hotly debates abortion, working mothers, and children's needs, scholars participate in, contribute to, and nuance conversations about feminism, women's agency, and normative family structures. Thus, in each chapter of this book, in addition to considering these ancient texts about mothers, I consider a contemporary example of maternal activism, in order to highlight the ways in which maternal self-sacrifice is a flexible discourse useful for a variety of political and ethical goals. These contemporary examples also, in turn, help shed light on new interpretive possibilities for understanding the ancient texts at the center of my study. Drawing on this analysis, I examine the ancient texts and the possible ways to describe how the rhetoric of the text uses maternal self-sacrifice to construct certain identities and promote particular beliefs.

Discourses about mothers and children are too often prescriptive and homogenizing; by recognizing that representations of mothers and children are produced for various reasons (and that the real-life experience of mothering is itself varied), this book nuances current conversations about both ancient and modern motherhood. As I show with regard to these textual mothers, a focused attention on mothers and their children does not necessarily lead to an improvement of the institution and experience of motherhood; instead, as Paula Cooey argues, these "cultural construals . . . romanticize motherhood and childhood, while demonizing [or harming] actual mothers."[6] Acknowledging a more complicated historical picture challenges scholars to take seriously the rhetorical flexibility and productivity of representations of mothers and children in wider cultural and politi-

---

Ellen Bradshaw Aitken, and Jonathan A. Draper (Minneapolis, MN: Fortress, 2008), 157–71.

[5] Melanie Johnson-DeBaufre, *Jesus among Her Children: Q, Eschatology, and the Construction of Christian Origins* (Cambridge, MA: Harvard University Press, 2005), 12–14.

[6] Paula M. Cooey, "'Ordinary Mother' as Oxymoron: The Collusion of Theology, Theory, and Politics in the Undermining of Mothers," in *Mother Troubles: Rethinking Contemporary Maternal Dilemmas*, ed. Julia E. Hanigsberg and Sara Ruddick (Boston: Beacon, 1999), 230.

cal conversations about women's agency and normative family structures, and to attend to their various political contexts and effects.

Maternal self-sacrifice is just one facet of the ways in which maternal figures are politically charged and rhetorically flexible. Feminists
have critiqued the expectation that mothers are naturally or ideally
self-sacrificing; in addition, the actions of a self-sacrificing mother have
been shown to be harmful to both mother and child, yet maternal
activists embrace certain losses and forms of suffering (indeed, even
sacrifices) as necessary paths toward creating a more livable, just future
for themselves and their children. These modern debates inform and
undergird discussions of ancient mothers, too; when scholars inquire
into ancient family structures, mother-child relationships, and wom-
en's roles, these contemporary issues and contexts are often necessarily
and inevitably part of the debate. Ancient conceptions of motherhood
did not connect maternity and self-sacrifice as naturally or immediately as contemporary US discourses do. Rather, in antiquity, the elite
materfamilias was typically imagined as formidable, distant from young
children, and influential in her adult children's lives. Only with the
introduction of discourses of martyrdom and self-sacrifice around the
turn of the era (first century BCE through third century CE), did a connection to maternity produce alternate (though not entirely distinct)
images of motherhood that utilized various forms of self-sacrifice.

Thinking about Ancient Motherhood

Establishing historical distance opens a space for disrupting the
easy use of the past as normative for the present, as well as for thinking critically about how representations of maternal sacrifice are both
contextual and flexible. As classicist Suzanne Dixon has argued, ancient
ideals about motherhood, so different from modern ones, should cause
modern people to qualify and nuance their own ideas about "normal"
or "natural" family relations. She especially counters the assumption
that a mother's relationship with her young child must be tender, close,
and doting, writing that "the nearest approach to our own [modern]
idea of maternal self-sacrifice" is only in "the figure of the mother who

xvi   Mary, Mother of Martyrs

aspires to have her children exceed her own learning."[7] As an example, Dixon references Horace: "If the rich man doesn't exactly despise the other, he tries to set him straight and treats him the way a hovering mother endeavors to make her child a wiser and better person than she [*mater plus quam se sapere et virtutibus esse priorem vult*]."[8] Even this modest hint of self-sacrifice is not strongly linked to mothers alone, however. Dixon adds, "in general such stock characteristics are shared by fathers and are quoted in relation to adult children as much as young ones."[9] Dixon's suggestion that the ideal of maternal self-sacrifice did not exist in Greco-Roman antiquity has largely found acceptance among classicists, who describe the elite *materfamilias* as formidable, involved in her adult children's lives, and valued for her reproductive capabilities.

Although I agree with Dixon's claim that people in antiquity did not know the ideal of maternal self-sacrifice, I do suggest that the seeds of a naturalized connection between motherhood and self-sacrifice so prevalent in later Christian tradition and cultures were sown in the context of the stories of violence and community suffering that served as vehicles for identity formation and contestation in ancient Judaism and Christianity. Because she is focused on elite Roman matrons, Dixon does not consider Jewish and Christian texts in her analysis. I argue below that the image of a mother who painfully produces a child was a useful rhetorical device in these texts for Jews and Christians wishing to distinguish themselves from other traditions in the larger Greco-Roman world and from each other. They were in the process of birthing, or being born, with all of the attendant pain, fear, loss, and joy. A maternal figure is particularly useful for thinking about and explaining painful, difficult origins.

Before I turn to the argument about what is distinctive in Jewish and Christian texts, I briefly discuss here three broad themes that are often linked to discussions of maternal bodies and roles across Greek, Roman, Jewish, and Christian texts. Here, I highlight some

---

[7] Suzanne Dixon, *The Roman Mother* (Norman: University of Oklahoma Press, 1988), 133.

[8] Horace, "To Lollius Maximus," in *The Epistles of Horace*, trans. David Ferry (New York: Farrar Straus Giroux, 2001), 90–91.

[9] Dixon, *Roman Mother*, 133.

of the social, rhetorical, and conceptual uses of motherhood in this ancient material. First, the mother's body, as container and conduit, is a key figure for thinking about both continuity and change over time; second, a mother, whose identity is explicitly connected to others (her children, their father), invites reflection on community relationships and identity formation; and third, in a mother, pain and (re)productivity are linked, especially in the image of childbirth, but also in the pathos or danger of a mother's connection to her children.

Mothers as Vessels of Continuity

Mothers are often portrayed as guaranteeing various kinds of continuity; the womb, in particular, is the location of a woman's role in ensuring the continuation of a family, nation, or empire. Just as the womb is the vessel for the child, the mother is a vessel for the continuity of the group. Indeed, the Hippocratic "corpus, as well as Aristotle's biological works, view women as mothers, responsible for the reproduction of the family and the *polis*, and as passive and amorphous material bodies, existing to produce children. In this evaluation, woman is but a uterus."[10] The ancient metaphors used for the womb are indicative of this implicit purpose of a woman's body: "sewer,"[11] "jug" or "jar,"[12] or hungry creature yearning to be fed.[13] Also prominent are metaphors related to cooking: the womb was like

---

[10] Ann Ellis Hanson, "The Medical Writers' Woman," in *Before Sexuality: The Construction of Erotic Experience in the Ancient Greek World*, ed. David M. Halperin, John J. Winkler, and Froma I. Zeitlin (Princeton, NJ: Princeton University Press, 1990), 312. Hanson is summarizing a position that Guilia Sissa, among others, has taken. See, for example, Giulia Sissa, *Greek Virginity* (Cambridge, MA: Harvard University Press, 1990).

[11] Tertullian quoting Marcion (*Against Marcion* 3.11). I have used the translation by Ernest Evans (Oxford: Clarendon Press, 1972). See also Jennifer Glancy, *Corporal Knowledge: Early Christian Bodies* (New York: Oxford University Press, 2010), 120–27.

[12] A popular metaphor from the Hippocratic corpus; see Hanson, "Medical Writers' Woman," 317; and Helen King, *Hippocrates' Woman: Reading the Female Body in Ancient Greece* (New York: Routledge, 1998), 26.

[13] Plato, *Timaeus*, 91b–c. See also Jean Jacques Aubert, "Threatened Wombs: Aspects of Ancient Uterine Magic," *Greek, Roman and Byzantine Studies* 30, no. 3 (1989): 421–49, quotation on 423. Soranus implies a similar view of the womb in his *Gynecology* 1.36. I have used the translation by Owsei Temkin (Baltimore: Johns Hopkins University Press, 1956).

an oven that would cook the seed, and according to Artemidorus, a husband's dreams related to a hearth or oven were said to portend a wife's pregnancy.[14] All of these metaphors connect the uterus to containment and growth, thus connecting women's bodies to both continuity and change.

The womb, when it was out of place and not properly (re)productive, presented a problem for both the woman's body and the social body; wombs, and thus women, were meant to grow children not move around of their own accord. If the womb was not sufficiently attended to—that is, by being kept moist with semen and occupied with a fetus—it might begin to move around the body in search of moisture; this affliction was known as a "wandering womb," a "catchall diagnosis for the illnesses of women."[15] This could lead to uterine suffocation, often affecting virgins or widows, the symptoms of which included "loss of voice, choking, gnashing of teeth, rolling of eyes."[16] The stability of a woman's uterus was tied to the stability of the woman's health and, indeed, to the stability and continuity of the social group.

Ancient debates about the morality and appropriateness of abortion likewise focused on the continuity of a family or nation. Unlike modern debates that focus on women's (or fetal) rights, ancient authors were concerned with the proper maintenance of the household and/or the empire. For example, when Ovid describes abortion in *Amores* 2.14, he focuses on the potential loss to "the race of men": "Who would have crushed proud Priam in Troy if Thetis had refused to deliver herself of her burden? Had Ilia availed herself of this option and slain the tiny twins in her swollen abdomen, Romulus and Remus could never have founded Rome."[17] These mothers ensured the production of famous, influential sons and thus the perpetuation of the larger group.

---

[14] King, *Hippocrates' Woman*, 33.

[15] Nancy Demand, *Birth, Death, and Motherhood in Classical Greece* (Baltimore, MD: Johns Hopkins University Press, 1994), 32.

[16] Hanson, "Medical Writers' Woman," 319.

[17] Ovid, *Love Poems, Letters, and Remedies of Ovid*, trans. David R. Slavitt (Cambridge, MA: Harvard University Press, 2011), 76–77.

The situation was somewhat different for "independent" women, whose offspring would not be considered legitimate (and thus were of less interest to the men potentially involved); their pregnancies would not continue a family line or produce new generations in a household in the same way. As Anise Strong has noted, "Prostitutes are frequently associated in ancient texts with contraceptives, abortifacients, and infant exposure," because pregnancy would hurt the livelihood of *hetairai*, performers, and prostitutes (more accurately, it would affect the income of their owners).[18] Even though the continuity of the family line is not at issue in such cases, the continuation of the woman's work and her owner's income is a concern. A famous example is first attested in the Hippocratic treatise *On the Nature of the Child*. The version from the Hippocratic Corpus describes how a performer athletically aborted an embryo:

> A kinswoman of mine owned a very valuable singer, who used to go with men. It was very important that this girl should not become pregnant and thereby lose her value. Now this girl had heard the sort of thing women say to each other—that when a woman is going to conceive, the seed remains inside her and does not fall out. She digested this information, and kept a watch. One day she noticed that the seed had not come out again. She told her mistress, and the story came to me. When I heard it, I told her to jump up and down, touching her buttocks with her heels at each leap. After she has done this no more than seven times, there was a noise, the seed fell out on the ground, and the girl looked at it in great surprise. (*On the Nature of the Child* 13)

Even here, the focus is often on women's bodies as they are connected to men's economic well-being.

---

[18] Anise K. Strong, "Working Girls: Mother-Daughter Bonds among Ancient Prostitutes," in *Mothering and Motherhood in Ancient Greece and Rome*, ed. Lauren Hackworth Petersen and Patricia Salzman-Mitchell (Austin: University of Texas Press, 2012), 123.

The so-called Augustan marriage laws promoted marriage and childbearing (especially for elites) as good for the empire, by giving material rewards for both and by penalizing unmarried persons over age twenty (for women) and twenty-five (for men). Two blocks of legislation were passed during Augustus's reign: the *lex Iulia de maritandis ordinibus* (18 BCE) and the *lex Papia Poppaea* (9 CE). They were "imperial attempts to influence family patterns and behavior" by penalizing celibacy, childlessness, and adultery; offering benefits to Roman citizens who married and produced children; and encouraging widows and divorcees to remarry.[19] The official encouragement of motherhood, along with motherhood's idealization, was not unrelated to either medical sources on conception and pregnancy or to philosophical considerations of exemplary mothers; if women (and men) had legal and economic reasons to reproduce, the focus on women as properly fecund is not surprising.

Politically involved Roman mothers often played important and rather visible roles in their families' public lives, even if only indirectly.[20] Certain mothers, such as Cornelia, mother of the Gracchi, were hailed as exemplary women because of the ways they shaped great leaders.[21] Cornelia is commemorated as a paradigmatically good mother, "embod[ying] all of the traditional Roman female virtues."[22] In Egypt, Cleopatra's role as a mother was contested by her political enemies, yet the connection between mothers and politics was in some ways familiar to Roman audiences: "Cleopatra's identification with Isis, a goddess known for her connection to motherhood and nurturing, thus sets the stage for the central role her children play in political life in Alexandria. . . . In Rome, as in Egypt, motherhood occupied a prominent, if sometimes problematic, place in the soci-

---

[19] Miriam Peskowitz, "'Family/ies' in Antiquity: Evidence from Tannaitic Literature and Roman Galilean Architecture," in *The Jewish Family in Antiquity*, ed. Shaye J. D. Cohen (Atlanta, GA: Scholars, 1993), 17.

[20] Prudence Jones, "*Mater Patriae*: Cleopatra and Roman Ideas of Motherhood," in Petersen and Salzman-Mitchell, *Mothering and Motherhood in Ancient Greece and Rome*, 173.

[21] Ibid.

[22] Judith P. Hallett, "Introduction: Cornelia and Her Maternal Legacy," *Helios* 33, no. 2 (Fall 2006): 139.

ety's understanding of its own origins."[23] Politically, "motherhood marks transitions," utilizing naturalizing metaphors of motherhood as a pivotal identity tied to both the past and the future.[24] Maternal figures secure a future for their children and, therefore, for their community.

Mothers Representing Communal Bonds

In antiquity, many maternal figures were linked with origin stories, community cohesion, and identity formation. Prudence Jones has shown the ways in which liminal maternal figures from Rome and Egypt connect motherhood with danger and power, especially in transitional moments. The mothers of Romulus and Remus, for example, are unlikely maternal figures but powerful symbols of the emergence of Rome:

> [Romulus and Remus] were born to a woman whom others attempted to prevent from being a mother and who was an unwilling mother herself after being raped by the god Mars. The first of the twins' substitute mothers, a she-wolf, was another unlikely nurturer. . . . The twins' second foster mother was a shepherd's wife. In the ancient world, the occupation of shepherd likewise carried with it connotations of wildness.[25]

The other examples that Jones uses, including the Sabine women, Lucretia, and Cleopatra, are larger-than-life figures who not only are mothers of individuals (usually sons) but also become mothers of the entire community or the nation in the retelling. In ancient medical texts, moral treatises, and material remains, women are frequently portrayed in a larger context that uses their maternity to reflect on a community's emergence, identity, and cohesion.

---

[23] Jones, "Mater Patriae," 172.
[24] Ibid.
[25] Ibid.

This is also the case in the Hebrew Bible, where mothers, especially mothers of sons, are connected to the continuation of the nation,
to the perpetuation of God's people.[26] The initial founding mother,
Eve, becomes a paradigmatic figure in later Jewish and Christian exe-
gesis, as she is "mother of all living" (Gen. 3:20) and, for Christians,
an initiator of original sin (see, for example, Irenaeus, *Against Heresies*
3.22). The barren woman motif in Genesis (in which a woman wants
to have a child, is unable to conceive, prays for divine intervention,
and bears a son against the odds) is one of the ways in which the
deity is portrayed as concerned about human affairs: God orches-
trates the continuation of God's people, even involving the divine
self in matters of human reproduction.[27] These founding maternal
figures and their wombs are, then, the location of God's initiation of
and provision for the nation; they represent the origin and cohesion
of the community amid difficult and unlikely circumstances.

Ancient moralists focused on the proper ordering of the household, including the *materfamilias*'s role within it. They saw the mother
not only as the biological source of offspring but also as a key figure in the offspring's upbringing and education. An elite mother was
expected to prioritize both the rearing of her children in their younger
years and their marriage and professional success as they aged.[28] In
the infamous Christian Testament texts in which women are exhorted
to submit to their husbands (often referred to as the *Haustafeln* texts),
the *materfamilias* is similarly located in a central place (see Eph. 5:22–
26:9; Col. 3:18–4:1; 1 Pet 2:18–3:6). The word *mother* is not used,
though the authors also have in mind the *materfamilias* when they
address women/wives (γυναῖκες) and parents (πατέρες).[29] The proper

---

[26] Here, I understand the Septuagint as a formative text that was available to Jews and
Christians in the Greco-Roman world; that is, I am not referring to the more ancient
Israelite and Judahite traditions reflected in the Hebrew Bible.

[27] The barren matriarchs of Genesis include Sarah (16–18, 21), Rebekah (25), and
Rachel (29–30); other barren mothers in the Hebrew Bible include the wife of
Manoah, mother of Samson (Judg. 13) and Hannah (1 Sam. 1–2). The deity is also
connected to conception in the stories of Eve (Gen. 3–4), Ruth, the Shunammite
woman (2 Kings 4), and, in the Christian Testament, Elizabeth and Mary (Luke 1–2).

[28] Dixon, *Roman Mother*, 28, 120, 220.

[29] James P. Hering, *The Colossian and Ephesian* Haustafeln *in Theological Context: An
Analysis of Their Origins, Relationship, and Message* (New York: Peter Lang, 2007), 221.

ordering and structuring of the *oikos* thus depends on the mother in relation to other parts of the household (husband and children).

Marriage was intended to produce children, so ancient medical theories of procreation and conception are closely tied to familial considerations. Indeed, "*matrimonium* means an institution for making mothers (*matres*)."[30] Thus, ancient medical texts about women focus overwhelmingly on relationships: pregnant mother and fetus, and mother-infant dyad. There is also some discussion of the aging process, but most of the mothers whom these texts consider are young women with young children.[31] Moreover, the metaphors they use for the womb and for generation are closely related to the ancient household. In addition to the metaphors "jar" and "jug" mentioned above, many ancient sources utilize agricultural metaphors, especially the notion of seeds, when considering pregnancy and conception. When discussing the relative contributions of the mother and father, ancient writers debated whether each parent contributed a seed (the "two-seed theory") or the father contributed a seed and the mother only nourished the seed (the "one-seed theory").[32] These seed metaphors are closely related to the theme of continuity discussed above. They also reflect on the relationships within the household: father and mother, mother and child.

Ancient discussions of pregnancy are often not so much about pregnancy or the mother as they are about the fetus and its survival: "Medicine is never neutral . . . [but] carries cultural values, including beliefs about the human body and about the roles and relative importance of different age/gender groups . . . [and about what] is abnormal and what is normal"; thus, medical sources about the constitution and development of a fetus provide crucial information about ancient views of women's roles and the importance of reproduction for the household and *polis*.[33] The boundaries between

---

[30] Susan Treggiari, quoted in Genevieve Liveley, "*Mater Amoris*: Mothers and Lovers in Augustan Rome," in Petersen and Salzman-Mitchell, *Mothering and Motherhood in Ancient Greece and Rome*, 190.

[31] King, *Hippocrates' Woman*, 9.

[32] Gwynn Kessler, *Conceiving Israel: The Fetus in Rabbinic Narratives* (Philadelphia: University of Pennsylvania Press, 2009), 110.

[33] King, *Hippocrates' Woman*, 114.

blood, seed, and milk, or between mother and fetus (or neonate) were permeable, and sometimes, medical discussions implied few distinctions at all.

Greek physicians agreed that the embryo absorbed its mother's menstrual blood and the fetus "was nourished by its mother's menses."[34] Then, menses was thought to transform into milk after birth. The discussions of milk demonstrate not just an interest in nutrition and health but also the relationships implied by such mutual giving and taking. Moreover, breast milk was thought to transmit various moral values, not just calories.[35] For example, the philosopher Favorinus stated, "Just as the power and nature of the seed are able to form likenesses of body and mind, so the qualities and properties of milk have the same effect" (*Attic Nights* 12.1.14).[36] For this reason, ancient moralists worried about the influence of wet nurses upon their charges. They often implied (or outright commanded!) that a mother ought to nurse her own child, just as mothers did in the good old days.[37] By the end of the first century CE, most upper-class mothers did not breastfeed their own babies (or at least, authors mention breastfeeding mothers in a way that makes this sound like an unusual occurrence).[38] The concern about who nursed a child was often framed in moralizing terms: Good mothers nursed their children (or should, at least, acquire a good wet nurse); bad mothers left their children with deficient caregivers.

As a material manifestation of the values that medical texts and Augustan marriage laws promulgated, the Ara Pacis Augustae in Rome

---

[34] Lesley Dean-Jones, *Women's Bodies in Classical Greek Science* (New York: Oxford University Press, 1994), 152–53, 200.

[35] King, *Hippocrates' Woman*, 143.

[36] Aulus Gellius attributed this quote to Favorinus. See Denise Kimber Buell, *Making Christians: Clement of Alexandria and the Rhetoric of Legitimacy* (Princeton, NJ: Princeton University Press, 1999), 63.

[37] See, for example, Favorinus, *Attic Nights* 12.1.17–23; cited in Buell, *Making Christians*, 123.

[38] Beryl Rawson, "The Roman Family," in *The Family in Ancient Rome: New Perspectives*, ed. Beryl Rawson (Ithaca, NY: Cornell University Press, 1986), 30. See also Keith Bradley, "Wet-Nursing at Rome: A Study in Social Relations," 201–29 in the same volume.

likewise presents and encourages idealized images of motherhood, childhood, and family life.[39] The Senate erected this altar to peace between 13 and 9 BCE to honor Augustus's safe return from military campaigns in Gaul and Spain.[40] The various panels demonstrate the "celebration of childbearing . . . incorporated into a more general vision of happiness," the "joy of motherhood and the blessings of offspring in the animal kingdom," and "the blessings of the new age, mirrored in an image of fertility."[41] The children of the imperial family are foregrounded on one of the panels that shows the pious imperial house sacrificing; Augustus consistently "offered himself as the greatest *exemplum* and tried in his private life and public appearance to be a constant advertisement for the *mores maiorum*," or ancestral customs.[42]

Mothers Used to Express Pathos

Ancient mothers were often used to represent productive pain; for example, Helen King has shown that Hippocratic medicine divided a woman's pain in childbirth "into that which was necessary to the process, and that which was excessive and needed to be treated."[43] Thus, if the laboring woman experienced *ponoi*, that was to be expected; if she experienced *odynai*, she must be given some relief.[44] The "normal" birthing body was thus explicitly linked with pain: Although she might experience abnormal, excessive pain, a mother was expected to labor in pain. Likewise, in Euripides's eponymous play, Medea famously compares childbirth with war: "I would rather stand three times in the front of battle than bear one child" (*Medea*, 250–51). The birthing process is one of the predominant ways that

---

[39] Funerary reliefs are another example of material remains that portray idealized forms of motherhood. See Lauren Hackworth Petersen and Patricia Salzman-Mitchell, "Introduction: The Public and Private Faces of Mothering and Motherhood in Classical Antiquity," in Petersen and Salzman-Mitchell, *Mothering and Motherhood in Ancient Greece and Rome*, 5–6, 9.

[40] Paul Zanker, *The Power of Images in the Age of Augustus* (Ann Arbor: University of Michigan Press, 1990), 120–21.

[41] Ibid., 176–77, 312.

[42] Ibid., 158–59.

[43] King, *Hippocrates' Woman*, 114.

[44] Ibid., 125–26.

Greco-Roman texts link motherhood with pain; certain Jewish and Christian texts connect motherhood and pain in a few other ways. Because the ancient Jewish and Christian texts considered in this book locate mothers in contexts of social violence, the maternal figures they imagine are often confronted with struggle, trauma, pain, and loss.

When Paul of Tarsus used maternal imagery for the creation, which is "longing for the revealing of the children of God" (Rom. 8:19), he utilized the idea of childbirth as purposeful pain, writing that "the whole creation has been groaning in labor pains [πᾶσα ἡ κτίσις συστενάζει καὶ συνωδίνει] until now; and not only the creation, but we ourselves, who have the first fruits of the Spirit, groan inwardly while we wait for adoption, the redemption of our bodies" (Rom. 8:22–23). The pain associated with motherhood is also linked to vulnerability, loss, threat, or danger in other contexts besides childbirth. Certain well-known dramas reflect on the vulnerability of mothers and their children in ways that are regularly commemorated and ritualized. A particularly famous example is the story of Demeter and Persephone in the Eleusinian mysteries.[45] The story of Medea, with its "complex and interrelated griefs" (including exile, death, loss of status, betrayal, and revenge) and the stories about Niobe and her children are other examples of narratives about motherhood and grief.[46]

One of the most poignant examples of a maternal figure evoking pathos is from Josephus's *Jewish War*. As he narrates the siege of Jerusalem and demonstrates the horrors of that particular moment in the war, he tells the story of Mary, daughter of Eleazar, who suffered in the famine, along with the rest of Jerusalem (6.201–13). After the leaders of the Jewish war effort (whom Josephus calls "the tyrants" or "rebels") plundered her property, she cursed them but found herself unable to find food for her family. "In any case," Josephus says, "it was by now impossible to get any [food], wherever you tried." He then focuses on Mary's condition as she committed an act of desperation: "Famine gnawed at her vitals, and the fire of rage was ever fiercer than

---

[45] Demand, *Birth, Death, and Motherhood in Classical Greece*, 24.
[46] Laura Salah Nasrallah, "Grief in Corinth: The Roman City and Paul's Corinthian Correspondence," in *Contested Spaces: Houses and Temples in Roman Antiquity and the New Testament*, ed. David L. Balch and Annette Weissenrieder (Tübingen: Mohr Siebeck, 2012), 126.

famine. So, driven by fury and want, she committed a crime against nature." She seized her nursing son and spoke to him, which is a striking moment in two ways: It is unusual in the *Jewish War* for a woman to give a speech, and for a speech to be addressed to a baby. As classicist Honora Howell Chapman says, "Josephus could have had Mary simply direct her words to the rebels, who were the source of her agony."[47] Instead, however, Mary said to her infant, "My poor baby, why should I keep you alive in this world of war and famine? Even if we live till the Romans come, they will make slaves of us; and anyway, hunger will get us before slavery does; and the rebels are crueler than both. Come, be food for me, and an avenging fury to the rebels, and a tale of cold horror to the world to complete the monstrous agony of the Jews." The Slavonic version of Josephus has her saying, "Go, my child, whence you came," and the Greek seems to evoke this, too, by using σπλάγχνα (6.204), the word for guts, innards, and, sometimes, womb. This baby grew and was nurtured inside his mother, and now his mother put the child back in her body and *he* fed *her*.

"With these words," Josephus continues, "she killed her son, roasted the body, swallowed half of it, and stored the rest in a safe place." When the rebels smelled the roasted meat, they immediately showed up, ready to kill her if she would not share the food with them. After revealing that it was her own child that she had cooked and eaten, Mary said to the rebels, "This is my own child, and my own handiwork. Eat, for I have eaten already. Do not show yourselves weaker than a woman, or more pitiful than a mother. But if you have pious scruples, and shrink away from human sacrifice, then what I have eaten can count as your share, and I will eat what is left as well." After this striking and shaming speech, the rebels "slunk away, trembling, not daring to eat, although they were reluctant to yield even this food to the mother" (6.212).

For Josephus, Mary represents the horrors of the war (and "the whole city" shudders with him) and the results of defying the Roman Empire. In her speech to her child, she said that the only possible outcomes for them were slavery and hunger, but she added, "The rebels are

---

[47] Honora Chapman, "Spectacle and Theater in Josephus's *Bellum Judaicum*" (PhD diss., Stanford University, 1998), 89.

crueler than both." Her "tale of cold horror" is also intended to shame
the Romans as particularly merciless and brutal. Caryn Reeder elaborates:

> According to Josephus, this suffering is the fault of the
> rebels (and is also compounded by the rebels; cf. *J.W.*
> 5.431–438). In line with the theology of Deuteronomy
> and Lamentations and with the interpretations of defeat
> in Greco-Roman historiographies, the people are pun-
> ished for rebellion against God and Rome by the capture,
> enslavement, starvation, and deaths of wives and children.
> Instead of having pity on the women and children (2.237,
> 400; 5.418), the rebels are pitiless in their treatment of the
> dying (4.384)—as indeed are the Romans as they indis-
> criminately slaughter and enslave women, children, and
> the elderly in punishment of the rebellion of men (2.494–
> 496, 3.132–134, 4.78, 6.271, etc.).[48]

Traditions about the Maccabean mother and her seven sons (see
chap. 3) draw heavily on stories like this one, which link motherhood,
suffering, protest, and the continuation of the Jewish nation amid
violent oppression. Josephus's Mary, like the Maccabean mother, also
serves as a shaming device for the male figures in the story: She told
them to eat her child, because she already had, and if they refused,
they would "show [themselves] weaker than a woman, or more pitiful than a mother."

In his *Sayings of Spartan Women*, Plutarch also ironically uses the
presumed weakness of mothers. The Spartan mothers, according to
Plutarch, were renowned for their tough parenting and national pride,
especially in wartime settings.[49] Famously, Spartan mothers sent their
sons off to war with shields that read "with it or on it" (*Moralia* 241F)—
meaning they should return victorious or dead. Other anecdotes from
Plutarch demonstrate Spartan women's single-minded commitment

---

[48] Caryn A. Reeder, "Pity the Women and Children: Punishment by Siege in Josephus's
Jewish War," *Journal for the Study of Judaism* 44, no. 2 (Spring 2013): 20.
[49] Mary Rose D'Angelo, "*Eusebeia*: Roman Imperial Family Values and the Sexual
Politics of 4 Maccabees and the Pastorals," *Biblical Interpretation* 11, no. 2 (2003): 148.

to Sparta: One killed her son when he dishonored Sparta (240F), and another forbid mourners for her son because he was not brave and therefore did not deserve to be mourned (241A). After her sons fled from the enemy to save their own lives, one mother lifted her skirts and asked, "Do you intend to hide in here from whence you came?" (241B), using the relative strength of the maternal body to shame her sons' weakness. The figure of Megisto, from Plutarch's *On the Bravery of Women*, also showed unusual bravery; when a tyrant wanted to kill her young child, the soldiers looked for the child among the other children. Megisto "called him by name [and] said, 'Come here, child, and before you can realize and think, be delivered from this bitter despotism; since for me it is more grievous to look upon your undeserved slavery than your death" (*Moralia* 252A–C). Plutarch's brave mothers and Josephus's cannibal mother behaved in extraordinary ways during war; the stories work by assuming a natural connection between mothers and their children and then disrupting that connection in unexpected ways (killing the child, shaming an adult son). That disruption evokes both surprise and pathos in the audience.

Although Plutarch and Josephus may have assumed that this connection between mothers and their children is "natural," however, historians of these ancient texts should be careful not to assume a natural, essential, and ahistorical link always existing between mothers and children. As one way to guard against that assumption, this book includes a consideration of contemporary maternal activists in every chapter. These maternal activists work in a variety of settings and for a variety of causes, but their deployment of their maternity for complex social, political, and ethical goals disrupts the easy assumptions often made about how mothers "naturally" feel and behave.

The Challenge of Maternal Activisms

Although much of the literature on maternal dilemmas related to self-sacrifice frames the debate in terms of *agency* and *choice* (important feminist values), the work of maternal activists challenges the individualized and privatized views of motherhood that populate contemporary discussions of (primarily elite) motherhood. Maternal

activists strategically essentialize motherhood as care, as concern for
the other. By doing so, they highlight particular struggles and promote
certain political goals. The connections between victimization and
agency are especially poignant in the work of maternal activists; thus,
contemporary maternal activists ensure that women's experience and
empowerment will not be understood in an atomized way but must
be seen in a larger social, political, economic, and familial context.

I consider recent examples of women from the United States, Latin
America, Russia, and the Middle East, all of whom strategically deploy
their motherhood for various activist goals. In each exegetical chapter,
I juxtapose the ancient maternal figure with an example of contemporary maternal activism: Mary is considered alongside the *madres de
Plaza de Mayo*, the women of Revelation are alongside women combatants from the Salvadoran civil war, the Maccabean mother is juxtaposed
with women suicide bombers in Israel and Palestine, and Perpetua and
Felicitas are considered alongside the women of Pussy Riot. These jux-
tapositions are not intended as straightforward comparisons but are
included to highlight the ways in which maternal self-sacrifice can be
understood as strategic, varied, politically charged, and rhetorically
flexible. Contemporary examples thus help us appreciate the complexity of the ancient texts at the center of this study and help us avoid
assuming that maternal self-sacrifice can bear only one meaning.

The Problem of Motherhood and Self-Sacrifice
A Feminist Problem

Conversations about motherhood are deeply connected to
notions of sacrifice and pain, which are often naturalized with reference to the discomfort of pregnancy, the labor of childbirth, and the
emotional and physical work of raising a child.[50] Feminist psycholo-

---

[50] For foundational work critiquing motherhood as exclusively linked to self-sacri-
fice, see Adrienne Rich, *Of Woman Born: Motherhood as Experience and Institution* (New
York: Norton, 1976). More recently, Andrea O'Reilly's work has pioneered mother-
hood studies as a field of academic inquiry; see her *Maternal Theory: Essential Readings*
(Toronto: Demeter, 2007); *Feminist Mothering* (Albany: State University of New York
Press, 2008); and *Twenty-First Century Motherhood: Experience, Identity, Policy, Agency*
(New York: Columbia University Press, 2010).

gist Carol Gilligan has presented one of the better-known critiques of feminine and motherly virtue as self-sacrifice; her "model of the morality of caring and connection has spawned a sizable literature [in psychology and social science] . . . . Most of them designate self-sacrifice as a defect."[51] Feminist scholars and activists in a variety of fields thus often find themselves in a double bind; leaving the connections between motherhood and self-sacrifice unchallenged means that mothers (and, by extension, all women) will be expected to gladly sacrifice for their children and for others, yet critiquing the "natural" association between motherhood and self-sacrifice can lead to charges that feminists are antifamily or antimother.

The seeds of the idea that mothers are naturally self-sacrificing may be in a variety of places; my book locates at least one of the seeds in the figure of the Virgin Mary, as a self-sacrificing mother who has been idealized throughout Christian history. My book thus attempts to address this double bind by considering formative texts in the New Testament and early Christianity, including texts about Mary, in which motherhood is linked with self-sacrifice; these texts neither prescribe maternal self-sacrifice as normative nor prohibit it, but instead use these discourses to reflect on other religious, political, ethnoracial, and philosophical issues.

A Theo-Ethical Problem

Feminist and womanist scholars in religion have long interrogated the connections made between women and self-denial; in Christian theology and ethics, this work has special significance because self-sacrifice has been "glorified in much of Christian piety," modeled on the example of Jesus.[52] Traditional Christian theology has often framed motherhood as a naturally self-sacrificing insti-

---

[51] Howard M. Bahr and Kathleen S. Bahr, *Toward More Family-Centered Family Sciences: Love, Sacrifice, and Transcendence* (New York: Lexington Books, 2010), 16. See Carol Gilligan, *In a Different Voice: Psychological Theory and Women's Development* (Cambridge, MA: Harvard University Press, 1982).
[52] Joanna Dewey, "Sacrifice No More," in *Distant Voices Drawing Near: Essays in Honor of Antoinette Clark Wire*, ed. Holly E. Hearon (Collegeville, MN: Liturgical Press, 2004), 170.

tution (and has therefore idealized women in general as naturally self-sacrificing). Indeed, Valerie Saiving's 1960 article "The Human Situation: A Feminine View," one of the foundational articles in Christian feminist theology, critiques the traditional notion of sin as self-assertion and love as agapic selflessness.[53] Saiving's article offers examples from a mother's experience. She famously started that article with these words: "I am a student of theology; I am also a woman."[54] Bonnie Miller-McLemore comments, "Few have added and embellished a sentence implicit in Saiving's essay itself: 'I am also a mother.' Failure to do so is a mistake, particularly during a time when the term *family values* has become a distorted and sometimes politically dangerous code word for reinstituting male dominance and female self-sacrifice."[55] Questioning the necessity and prescription of women's sacrifice has thus been a key part of Christian feminist theology, which tends to argue that sacrificial theologies "legitimat[e] hierarchy, encourag[e] violent behavior, and glorif[y] innocent victimhood."[56]

A range of feminist, womanist, and mujerista work has also recognized the potential power and political usefulness of self-sacrifice, however. For example, Anna Mercedes focuses on the ways in which "self-giving, or *kenosis*, can also function as a resistance strategy against patriarchy and other forms of oppression."[57] Her argument attends to the contexts of women's sacrificial work and the ways in which self-giving can be life-giving:

> The feminist claim that sacrifice and service wrongly consume many women's lives holds significant political impact in its sweeping accuracy. . . . Yet the claim that it is unilaterally wrong for service to characterize people's lives

---

[53] Valerie Saiving, "The Human Situation: A Feminine View," *Journal of Religion* 40, no. 2 (1960): 100–112.

[54] Ibid., 100.

[55] Bonnie Miller-McLemore, *Also a Mother: Work and Family as Theological Dilemma* (Nashville, TN: Abingdon, 1994), 84.

[56] Dewey, "Sacrifice No More," 159.

[57] Anna Mercedes, *Power For: Feminism and Christ's Self-Giving* (New York: T & T Clark, 2011), 2. This work is based on her dissertation, "Passionate Christ: *Kenosis*, Feminism, and Desire" (PhD diss., Drew University, 2009).

overlooks the complexity of human experience, forgetting the people—women included—who choose service precisely as an expression of their own rich character, and also minimizing the extent to which all lives, male and female, are embedded in layers of dependency and caregiving. This last point has been particularly emphasized in womanist and Latina feminist work, where community and care have often been readily affirmed as good and life-giving, and indeed as necessary for survival.[58]

As Mercedes acknowledges, sacrificial models are still troubling to many feminists, because a retrieval of self-sacrifice as a positive resource in Christian theology risks revalorizing and essentializing women's sacrifice. Seeing *kenosis* in its complexity, including the relevance of particular contexts, works against a sweeping claim that all forms of women's self-sacrifice are damaging. In this book, I attempt to recognize maternal self-sacrifice as a potential space of resistance for women experiencing violence, without celebrating or reinscribing sacrifice as normative for all women.

A Historical Problem

The enterprise of women's history has often been critiqued for its emphasis on "retrieving" ancient women and/or their experiences, a task rendered difficult by the theoretical complexity of the relationship between the social world and texts, in addition to the dearth of relevant sources on women's lives in particular. Taking this challenge seriously, many historians have focused on representations of women because the figure of "woman" is accessible in the texts and because gendered discourses shaped the ancient social world, as they shape our own. As Judith Perkins says, "Although discourses do not represent 'reality,' they do have very real effects. In every society, persons come to understand themselves, their roles and their world through

---

[58] Mercedes, *Power For*, 6.

their culture's discursive practices and the 'reality' these practices bring into cultural consciousness."[59]

Attention to the representation of women has also opened up examinations of how discourses about women are often about something else; for example, as Kate Cooper has shown, "If we allow that many ancient accounts of female behavior are shaped rhetorically to suit a judgment of a male character, this means that their reflection of reality is distorted."[60] Likewise, I do not attempt to access the "real" women—for example "the historical Mary" or "the real Perpetua"—behind the texts but rather am highlighting the ways in which representations of these maternal figures have a variety of effects, both in antiquity and in contemporary scholarship.

Scholars working on social histories of the ancient family and household have emphasized that certain ideals were promulgated as normative, even officially rewarded, while others were dismissed as deviant or harmful; an understanding of these ideals, norms, and laws is crucial for contextualizing narratives that depict families, including mothers and their children. It is important to note, however, that the stakes of these discussions are high; "few if any areas of study have been so politically, ideologically and emotionally sensitive as the study of the family."[61] When scholars make claims about ancient families, including what ancient people may or may not have felt about their families, they are also frequently moralizing about what is normal, natural, and expected in families throughout time, including modern families. Thus, although scholarship on the ancient household is crucial because it highlights the lives and roles of women, slaves, and children—who are often occluded in ancient texts and in historical scholarship—we must attend to the rhetorical work of "the family" in both ancient and scholarly texts. Self-sacrificing maternal figures, especially, are textual sites with pernicious effects.

---

[59] Judith Perkins, *The Suffering Self: Pain and Narrative Representation in the Early Christian Era* (New York: Routledge, 1995), 3.

[60] Kate Cooper, *The Virgin and the Bride: Idealized Womanhood in Late Antiquity* (Cambridge, MA: Harvard University Press, 1996), 13.

[61] Halvor Moxnes, "What is Family?" in *Constructing Early Christian Families: Family as Social Reality and Metaphor*, ed. Halvor Moxnes (London: Routledge, 1997), 14.

CHAPTER 1

Agency, Submission, and Motherhood: Mary in the Canonical Gospels

My investigation of maternal self-sacrifice in early Christianity begins with Mary, the mother of Jesus, because she is a paradigmatic figure in the West, in both her mothering and her self-denial. Traditional Mariology presents the mother of Jesus as "the pure, self-sacrificing, humble handmaiden of the Lord and patient mother full of sorrows"; these virtues, moreover, are presented as aspirational ideals for all mothers, indeed all women.[62] Feminist scholars have rightly warned that this traditional image of Mary promotes women's passivity and domesticity, in addition to elevating biological motherhood as the primary (and often only) role for all women. Interrogating the connections among Mary, motherhood, and self-sacrifice has been an important and necessary facet of feminist interpretations of Mary. I build on that work in a way that also rejects the abusive use of Mary as a self-sacrificing mother, but I do so in a way that acknowledges the creative deployment of the same figure in struggles for justice; in doing so, I highlight the strategic use of Mary as sacrificial mother instead of seeing the connections among Mary, motherhood, and sacrifice as natural or assumed. When carefully held together, both interpretations (the harmful, abusive use of Mary and the creative, strategic use) allow us to see familiar biblical texts differently and to examine the various results of scholars' interpretive choices.

---

[62] Elisabeth Schüssler Fiorenza, *Jesus: Miriam's Child, Sophia's Prophet: Critical Issues in Feminist Christology* (New York: Continuum, 1994), 165.

In this consideration of Mary, I focus primarily on canonical infancy and crucifixion narratives, textual moments in which violence (or the threat of violence) is invoked in Mary's life.[63] Scholars often privilege those texts when discussing Mary as an idealized, self-sacrificing mother, thus creating and evaluating a composite image of Mary across the gospels. This composite image often glosses over or completely ignores the gospel texts that portray Jesus at odds with his mother and other family members (e.g., Mark 3:20–35 and parallels; Luke 2:41–52; sometimes John 2:1–11). I am especially interested in the ways in which this composite Marian image is mobilized by contemporary scholars who are engaging various modern sociopolitical, theological, and ethical debates; thus, I begin with this harmonized image of Mary, focusing on the ways in which she is both an idealized figure and an incredibly flexible one. Then I discuss some of the key features of traditional Mariology (including developments from the Reformation era and the Second Vatican Council), especially noting the connections between Mariology and women's subjectivity. A key concern of many feminist interpreters of Mary is the way that Mariology can have a strongly negative impact on women's lives.[64] Devotion to Mary, as well as creative deployment of Marian traditions, can also inspire bold social critique and movements of solidarity, as my discussion of the use of Mary by the *madres de Plaza de Mayo* also shows.

One current scholarly conversation about Mary emerges from Reformation (and Vatican II) discussions—namely, seeing Mary as an ideal disciple. A second major scholarly debate emerges from the women's movement: that is, the question of Mary's agency and

---

[63] The editors of Mary in the New Testament give consideration to each canonical text related to Mary (including even more tangential ones, such as Gal. 4:4 or Phil. 2:6–11). See Raymond E. Brown, Joseph A. Fitzmyer, Karl P. Donfried, and John Reumann, eds., *Mary in the New Testament: A Collaborative Assessment by Protestant and Roman Catholic Scholars* (Philadelphia: Fortress, 1978). The canonical texts that mention Mary (or "the mother of Jesus") are Matt. 1–2; Luke 1–2; Mark 3:31–35 and Synoptic parallels; Mark 6:3 and parallels; John 2:1–12; John 19:25–7; and Acts 1:14.

[64] See, for example, Barbara Corrado Pope, "Immaculate and Powerful: The Marian Revival in the Nineteenth Century," in *Immaculate and Powerful: The Female in Sacred Image and Social Reality* (Boston: Beacon, 1985), 173–200.

consent, especially in the Annunciation (Luke 1:26–38). After discussing each of these interpretive debates, including the questions that are asked, the lenses that are utilized, and the ways these debates engage contemporary concerns, I consider an alternate contemporary debate: maternal activists' use of sacrificial metaphors and images. Specifically, I focus on the *madres de Plaza de Mayo*, who creatively deploy notions of maternal self-sacrifice and Marian devotion in their activist work in Argentina. This discussion of the *madres'* strategic use of Mary sets up a consideration of three key biblical texts about Mary that involve suffering, loss, violence, and maternity, and it leads us to a greater appreciation of these texts' complexity.

For most interpreters, the Annunciation (Luke 1:26–38) is a key text for deciding whether Mary is an active agent and participant in the divine plan or a self-sacrificing, humble "servant of the Lord"; other texts, such as Matthew's infancy narrative (Matt 1:18–2:23) and John's crucifixion scene (John 19:25–27), sometimes earn consideration in these discussions, as Mary's maternity is intertwined with risk and death. After focusing on each of these texts in turn, I discuss how attending to the complexity of these various representations and their multiple rhetorical contexts allows both for an interrogation of the risks of the concept of maternal self-sacrifice and for an identification of the highly contextual (if also complex) possibilities for promoting women's flourishing. The figure of Mary, especially as a suffering, self-sacrificing mother, does diverse kinds of rhetorical work for interpreters and is produced for various reasons in both ancient texts and modern debates.

Mother Mary, Quite Contrary

Various narratives about Mary in the New Testament describe her at her son's birth and death, particularly grave moments for a mother. From these narrative fragments, both traditional Mariology and biblical scholarship on Marian texts produce a composite, seamless vision of Mary, sometimes coterminous with an imagined historical Mary. As Elizabeth Johnson has noted, "Traditional Mariology achieved a synthesized view of Mary by harmonizing the diverse gospel texts into a smooth-running narrative of her life, sometimes even rounding things out by adding the postbiblical doctrines of the Immaculate Conception at the beginning and the Assumption at the end."[65] Like traditional Mariology, contemporary biblical scholars and theologians combine the disparate brief suggestive references to Mary in the New Testament into a coherent image of Jesus's mother. The tendency to combine the stories, to create a mosaic using each narrative tile, is understandable; indeed, interpreters make similar moves with Jesus, Peter, Mary Magdalene, and other New Testament figures.[66] In addition, when scholars do not clearly distinguish literary, historical, and theological interests, arguments, and ideas, it becomes easy to weave together the separate texts about Mary into a composite picture.

In Mary's case, the coherent image produced heightens the emotional connections of her interpreters to a sacrificing, grieving, suffering mother. The connection of mothers, particularly suffering mothers, to productive fecundity makes Mary an ideal figure for projection, identification, and desire. Ultimately, however, the desire to produce a seamless narrative of Mary does violence to the variety of images presented in the New Testament—and, more importantly, may occlude the various contexts in which Mary is used, and the varied results of her image being mobilized. That is, smoothing over the differences among the gospel narratives risks ignoring the contingent nature of the construction—and thus the reasons for and results of constructing it. Rather than highlighting the constructed nature of the image (and the reasons for and results of constructing it), many see the "real" Mary.[67] The literary Mary becomes coterminous with the historical and theological Mary, such that discussions

---

[65] Elizabeth A. Johnson, *Truly Our Sister: A Theology of Mary in the Communion of Saints* (New York: Continuum, 2003), 211.

[66] For Johnson's metaphor of tesserae in a mosaic, see ibid., and Elizabeth A. Johnson, *Dangerous Memories: A Mosaic of Mary in Scripture* (New York: Continuum, 2004).

[67] Scot McKnight even indicates this in his title *The Real Mary: Why Evangelical Christians Can Embrace the Mother of Jesus* (Brewster, MA: Paraclete, 2007). In addition, the biographical approaches to Mary have a similar emphasis on the "real" person of Mary; see, for example, Michael Jordan, *Mary: The Unauthorised Biography* (London: Weidenfeld & Nicolson, 2001) and Lesley Hazleton, *Mary: A Flesh-and-Blood Biography of the Virgin Mother* (New York: Bloomsbury, 2004).

about what Mary would have experienced, believed, felt, or thought seem misleadingly about a *real* person instead of a historical figure or literary character. Perhaps the most troubling aspect of this move to describe the "real" Mary is the way in which she is so often presented as not only an idealized woman but also an idealized mother. Feminist scholarship on modern motherhood has demonstrated the problems with presenting a single vision of motherhood as an unchanging, often impossible, ideal.[68] Ideals are, of course, necessary but "can be destructive when invested with ultimacy and absolutism," especially where family is concerned.[69] Feminist scholars have often pointed to Mary—both mother and virgin—as the paradigmatic impossible ideal.

Acknowledging that the figure of Mary is different in each gospel context resists the tendency to assign Mary a distinct, definite, unchanging identity; if we accept the various portraits of Mary as distinct, then we can more easily see the diverse work that the figure of Mary as a self-sacrificing mother does for interpreters. Her image is used to tell a variety of stories—about discipleship, parenthood, devotion, and sacrifice. By examining the multiple rhetorical contexts in which each text invokes Mary's body and story, we are able to see the stakes of the image: that is, Mary's maternal self-sacrifice is often used in service of women's oppression, yet it also opens certain possibilities for transgressive and powerful social critique.

Mary's interpreters have already acknowledged the rhetorical flexibility of Mary's constructed composite image, which has in turn prompted reflection on the reasons for her flexibility.[70] Theologians and biblical scholars point to her committed discipleship, her

---

[68] See, for example, Rich, *Of Woman Born*; Anne Carr and Elisabeth Schüssler Fiorenza, eds., *Motherhood: Experience, Institution, Theology* (Edinburgh: T & T Clark, 1989); Molly Ladd-Taylor and Lauri Umansky, eds., *"Bad" Mothers: The Politics of Blame in Twentieth-Century America* (New York: New York University Press, 1998); Hanigsberg and Ruddick, *Mother Troubles*; and Cristina Grenholm, *Motherhood and Love: Beyond the Gendered Stereotypes of Theology* (Grand Rapids, MI: Eerdmans, 2011).

[69] Bonnie Miller-McLemore, "Ideals and Realities of Motherhood: A Theological Perspective," in Hanigsberg and Ruddick, *Mother Troubles*, 295.

[70] Diego Irarrazaval, Susan Ross, and Marie-Theres Wacker, eds., *The Many Faces of Mary*, Concilium 2008, no. 4 (London: SCM, 2008).

motherhood, or the power of the Eternal Feminine.[71] Psychologist Shari Thurer suggests that the brief references to Mary in the canonical texts represent "an inauspicious beginning, to say the least, but it provided a lot of room for invention. Here we have practically a blank screen, a perfect canvas for our projections."[72] Rather than asking *why* Mary is such a flexible figure, I suggest focusing on a different set of questions: For what purpose is Mary's image being used? What notions of motherhood and/or sacrifice are invoked? Who benefits from the interpretation? Who is harmed?

In Mary, we see perhaps the most obvious example of the flexibility of maternal self-sacrifice. The various narratives about her cannot be distilled easily into one seamless narrative, nor can her character be summarized by one particular descriptor, but she could instead be used as an occasion to reflect on the results of various interpretations. Rather than idealizing or valorizing Mary as a suffering mother, scholars could use her narratives to prompt the acknowledgment of other mothers' suffering in various contexts. Furthermore, interpretations of Mary could highlight the complexities of responses to suffering and oppression, instead of prescribing one particular response as normative. In doing so, interpreters would acknowledge both the complexities of the different texts about Mary and the various ways that those texts have been interpreted in service of liberatory (and oppressive) goals.

Traditional Mariology emphasizes Mary's passivity, virginity, and humility. She is typically described as "the pure, self-sacrificing, humble handmaiden of the Lord and patient mother full of

---

[71] For an example of an interpreter who attributes Mary's "remarkable plasticity" to her committed discipleship, see Raymond E. Brown, *The Birth of the Messiah: A Commentary on the Infancy Narratives in the Gospels of Matthew and Luke*, updated ed. (New York: Doubleday, 1993), 318n66. Miller-McLemore attributes this phenomenon to Mary's motherhood ("Pondering All These Things," in *Protestant Perspectives on Mary*, ed. Beverly Roberts Gaventa and Cynthia Rigby (Louisville, KY: Westminster John Knox, 2002), 99). Pelikan and Zervos reflect on the appeal of the Eternal Feminine; see Jaroslav Pelikan, *Mary through the Centuries: Her Place in the History of Culture* (New Haven, CT: Yale University Press, 1996), 216–17, and George Themelis Zervos, "Christmas with Salome," in *A Feminist Companion to Mariology*, ed. Amy-Jill Levine and Maria Mayo Robbins (Cleveland, OH: Pilgrim, 2005), 98.

[72] Shari Thurer, *Myths of Motherhood: How Culture Reinvents the Good Mother* (New York: Penguin, 1995), 107.

sorrows"—virtues extolled for all women by patriarchal societies and religious communities.[73] As mother of a crucified messianic figure and a classic model of traditional femininity, Mary is hailed both for her submission to God's plan (especially at the Annunciation) and for enduring (even accepting) the violent death of her son. Because Mary is one of the prominent female figures (if not *the* primary female figure) in the Christian tradition, her role in the gospels and later devotional traditions is crucial for understanding women's subjectivity in the West.[74] As Schüssler Fiorenza has noted, "Whereas the [Roman Catholic Church] hierarchy is said to represent Christ's masculinity and God's father power, all so-called lay Christians, men and wo/men, are exhorted to imitate Mary, who perfectly represents the feminine qualities of receptivity, subordination, humility, malleability, obedience, and passivity."[75] John Paul II, in his 1987 encyclical on Mary in the life of the church, connected the figure of Mary to feminine virtues:

> Femininity has a unique relationship with the Mother of the Redeemer, a subject which can be studied in greater depth elsewhere. Here I simply wish to note that the figure of Mary of Nazareth sheds light on womanhood as such by the very fact that God, in the sublime event of the Incarnation of his Son, entrusted himself to the ministry, the free and active ministry of a woman. It can thus be said that women, by looking to Mary, find in her the secret of living their femininity with dignity and of achieving their own true advancement. In the light of Mary, the Church sees in the face of women the reflection of a beauty which

---

[73] Schüssler Fiorenza, *Jesus: Miriam's Child*, 165.

[74] Ibid., 171, and Johnson, *Truly Our Sister*, 3.

[75] *Jesus: Miriam's Child*, 171. Schüssler Fiorenza writes "wo/men" with a slash to "indicate that the category of 'wo/man-wo/men' is a social construct. Wo/men are not a unitary social group but are fragmented by structures of race, class, ethnicity, religion, sexuality, colonialism, and age. This destabilization of the term 'wo/men' underscores the differences between wo/men and within individual wo/men. This writing is inclusive of subaltern men who in kyriarchal systems are seen 'as wo/men' and functions as a linguistic corrective to androcentric language use" (*Wisdom Ways: Introducing Feminist Biblical Interpretation* [Maryknoll, NY: Orbis, 2001], 216).

mirrors the loftiest sentiments of which the human heart is capable: the self-offering totality of love; the strength that is capable of bearing the greatest sorrows; limitless fidelity and tireless devotion to work; the ability to combine penetrating intuition with words of support and encouragement.[76]

By connecting womanhood and femininity with an idealized vision of Mary, traditional Mariology sets the mother of Jesus on a pedestal and sets women up for failure; it is impossible to embody all of her virtues, to say nothing of being both virgin *and* mother.

Even though Marian doctrine and devotion are often thought to be the sole domain of the Roman Catholic Church, the influence of Mariology is evident in other Christian traditions. George Themelis Zervos emphasizes the ambiguous results of Marian doctrine and devotion in the Eastern Orthodox Church:

> The image of Mary as the archetypal self-sacrificing woman functioned within this system partially as a mechanism of control over women. For it was this image, worshiped and emulated by women through their lives, that also taught them to be submissive: "Let it be done to me according to thy word" (Lk. 1.38). But one might also argue that this image of Mary served women well as a model of dignified acquiescence in the face of the overwhelming power wielded by the patriarchal religions.[77]

The overwhelming influence of the Virgin Mother as paradigmatic self-sacrificing woman crosses other denominational and cultural lines, even though Protestants are often characterized by their deliberate evasion of Mary.[78] Especially in certain European Reformed

---

[76] John Paul II, *Redemptoris Mater* [Encyclical on the Blessed Virgin Mary in the Life of the Pilgrim Church], March 25, 1987, sec. 46, http://w2.vatican.va/content/john-paul-ii/en/encyclicals/documents/hf_jp-ii_enc_25031987_redemptoris-mater.html.
[77] Zervos, "Christmas with Salome," 98.
[78] Miller-McLemore calls this Protestant "abstinence" from Mary ("Pondering All These Things," 97–114).

traditions, "Mary became the *model of motherhood* and *the archetype of the ideal woman*, who displays the gentle feminine virtues that are essential to the civilizing of men and nations."[79] This civilizing impulse of Marian devotion is thus twofold, evidenced in both the conquistadors who conquered "under the standard of Mary"[80] (and in various dictatorial regimes in Latin America ever since, as the laity are encouraged to imitate Mary's selflessness, acquiescence, and obedience) and in discourses of *marianismo*, which "holds the woman as morally superior to the man on the basis of her humility and self-sacrifice, . . . praying for the souls of her sinful menfolk to whom she is nonetheless submissive."[81]

Nevertheless, "popular cults of Mary have had a tremendous attraction for the downtrodden and exploited," and some feminists have idealized "her as one who embodies and personifies the oppressed who are being liberated."[82] Feminists, especially Catholic feminists, have long emphasized that Mary has been used in service of institutional oppression, even while the potential exists for Marian reflection to be used for liberatory goals. Els Maeckelberghe summarizes the impasse this way:

> [Mary] is an ambiguous religious symbol. She has evoked
> strong emotions in the faithful throughout centuries of
> Christianity. She has been a model for women and men,
> but the ambiguity has been especially devastating for
> women. On the one hand, womanhood was elevated in

---

[79] Daniel L. Migliore, "Woman of Faith: Toward a Reformed Understanding of Mary," in *Blessed One: Protestant Perspectives on Mary*, ed. Beverly Roberts Gaventa and Cynthia Rigby (Louisville, KY: Westminster John Knox, 2002), 119; see also Miller-McLemore, "Pondering All These Things."

[80] Clodovis Boff, "Toward a Social Mariology," in Irarrazaval, Ross, and Wacker, *Many Faces of Mary*, 47.

[81] Marguerite Guzman Bouvard, *Revolutionizing Motherhood: The Mothers of the Plaza de Mayo* (Wilmington, DE: Scholarly Resources, 1994), 184. For an exploration of the connections between marriage and "being civilized," see Nancy F. Cott, *Public Vows: A History of Marriage and the Nation* (Cambridge, MA: Harvard University Press, 2000).

[82] Jane Schaberg, *The Illegitimacy of Jesus: A Feminist Theological Interpretation of the Infancy Narratives*, expanded twentieth anniversary ed. (Sheffield, England: Sheffield Phoenix, 2006), 25.

> Mary; on the other hand it was impossible for women to be like Mary. The ideal of simultaneous virginity and motherhood was an impossible one. It nevertheless did not refrain [sic] women from praying to Mary, going on pilgrimages to Marian shrines, seeking comfort in chapels devoted to Mary. It seems that Mary is more than an oppressive image.[83]

To say that Mariology is always oppressive to women, then, would be to suggest that women have no idea what is good for them. Highlighting this ambivalent reality, in which Mariology is strongly connected to both women's oppression and the potential of women's flourishing, throws into sharp relief the various ends toward which a flexible and productive image of maternal sacrifice can be put.

Certain discussions in the Protestant Reformation about Mary and women's roles prefigured later developments in the Roman Catholic Church, especially at Vatican II. Reformers emphasized Mary's place among the faithful and rejected any interpretation of Mary that suggested she was a mediator between humans and the divine.[84] Several dogmatic declarations in the nineteenth and twentieth centuries expanded Mary's role in salvation, but the Second Vatican Council constricted Mary's importance; after much debate, the consideration of Marian devotion was placed within the document on ecclesiology, *Lumen Gentium*, instead of in its own separate document. According to Philip Endean, "Taking a lead from the council's decision to incorporate Mary within the Dogmatic Constitution on the Church, [many modern Catholic writers] have tended simply to present Mary as the pre-eminent Christian disciple, effectively as St Mary the Virgin rather than as Mother of God."[85] This post–Vatican II approach mirrors some Reformation concerns,

---

[83] Els Maeckelberghe, *Desperately Seeking Mary: A Feminist Appropriation of a Traditional Religious Symbol* (Kampen, The Netherlands: Pharos, 1991), 3.

[84] Migliore, "Woman of Faith," 117–18.

[85] Philip Endean, introduction to "The Fundamental Principle of Marian Theology by Karl Rahner," in *Mary: The Complete Resource*, ed. Sarah Jane Boss (London: Oxford University Press, 2007), 292.

as reformers and the churches that have followed them also tend to claim Mary simply as a model disciple.[86] These emphases address and develop certain doctrinal conversations from the Reformation era, especially concerning Christology and soteriology. These issues also feature prominently in modern scholarship on Mary, as interpreters emphasize her discipleship, faithfulness, and openness to the divine will.

Raymond Brown, Charles Talbert, and other well-known New Testament scholars have argued that we ought to consider Mary the first and ideal Christian[87] disciple because she responds positively to the "gospel" of Jesus's impending birth.[88] In recent biblical scholarship, especially for Catholic scholars, "Mary's discipleship rather than motherhood has been subject of Catholic mariology and more especially, of Marian devotional writing."[89] John van den Hengel, SCJ, who attempts to retrieve the symbolism of Mariology for use in the contemporary church (not in a reactionary way, as he faults many current devotees of Mary), gives a summary that is paradigmatic of the harmonization of gospel accounts in this project and the idealization of Mary's discipleship: "Mary was the woman who prepared to be a disciple of her own son. Jesus became the teacher of his mother from the Temple to Cana to the cross. Nowhere does Mary refuse to learn; nowhere is she shown as separate from Jesus. She is the face of the follower of Jesus, of the perfect community of disciples, the Church. She is the measure of the

---

[86] Miller-McLemore, "Pondering All These Things", and Lois Malcolm, "What Mary Has to Say about God's Bare Goodness," in Gaventa and Rigby, *Blessed One*, 131–44.

[87] Few have interrogated the troubling assumption that Mary is a Christian or represents Christian discipleship; since we can hardly speak of Christianity in Jesus's own lifetime, let alone before his conception, we need better vocabulary for assessing Mary's relative obedience, response, and action.

[88] Brown et al., *Mary in the New Testament*, 125–26; Brown, *Birth of the Messiah*, 318–19; Charles H. Talbert, *Reading Luke: A Literary and Theological Commentary on the Third Gospel* (New York: Crossroad, 1982), 22–24; also see Janice Capel Anderson, "Mary's Difference: Gender and Patriarchy in the Birth Narratives," *Journal of Religion* 67, no. 2 (April 1987): 192.

[89] Sarah Jane Boss, *Mary* (New York: Continuum, 2004), 57. Though it is not her focus, Boss's emphasis on Mary's motherhood (instead of discipleship) is one way to avoid the problematic assumption that Mary is the prototype of the *Christian* believer.

Christian whose norm is Christ. As mother and believer she is to us a word about God."[90]

This focus is not found only in Catholic and/or devotional writing; Beverly Roberts Gaventa, writing as a Protestant, says, "At the risk of harmonizing these accounts [that is, the canonical gospels], I would propose that each of them is consistent with the identification of Mary as a disciple of Jesus."[91] In his interpretation of John 19, evangelical scholar Ben Witherington psychologizes Mary in a way that also seems to reference the Lukan Annunciation scene: "Mary learns that she is to be a mother as a disciple, not a mother and also a disciple. Discipleship must be the larger context in which her role as mother is delimited and defined. Mary responds in silence and submission. She obeys the word of the Lord and goes with the beloved disciple. In so doing she is the model woman—a testimony to a woman's new freedom in faith and also to a woman's traditional roles of serving under the authority and headship of man."[92] Even though John 19:25–27 says nothing about gender roles or discipleship (and neither the Beloved Disciple nor Mary responds to Jesus), Witherington emphasizes Mary's silence, submission, and womanly service as exemplary of her discipleship—and her mothering.

Simone de Beauvoir famously criticized the image of a mother kneeling at her son's feet as one of the most problematic aspects of Mariology and Christian theology; it is, she said, "the supreme masculine victory . . . the rehabilitation of woman through the

---

[90] John van den Hengel, "Miriam of Nazareth: Between Symbol and History," in Levine and Robbins, *Feminist Companion to Mariology*, 146. Similarly, in the introduction to *Blessed One*, Gaventa and Rigby say, "Mary also resists expectations by escaping the manger scene in Bethlehem and becoming a witness to the scandal of the cross" (p. 2).

[91] Beverly Roberts Gaventa, "'All Generations Will Call Me Blessed': Mary in Biblical and Ecumenical Perspective," in Levine and Robbins, *Feminist Companion to Mariology*, 129. See also the chapter on Luke's Mary, entitled "Disciple, Prophet, and Mother: Mary in Luke-Acts," in Beverly Roberts Gaventa, *Mary: Glimpses of the Mother of Jesus* (Columbia: University of South Carolina Press, 1995), 49–78.

[92] Ben Witherington, *Women in the Ministry of Jesus: A Study of Jesus' Attitudes to Women and Their Roles as Reflected in His Earthly Life* (New York: Cambridge University Press, 1984), 95.

accomplishment of her defeat."[93] Even though the modern project is to show what a devoted *disciple* Mary was, the result may still look very traditional, as Mary symbolizes the submissive mother/disciple learning from her son/Lord. Moreover, like other approaches to Mary's identity in the New Testament and her role in Christian theology, the image of Mary as disciple of her son presents her as idealized and exemplary in every way.

Another key site of interpretive debate concerns Mary's agency and freedom. Traditional Mariology typically emphasizes Mary's role as an open vessel, a willing container for the divine; Karl Rahner, for example, explained the doctrine of Mary's perpetual virginity thus: "Because her whole existence, all that she was throughout her life, from her conception to her death, was totally absorbed into this function of being the mother of God; *because apart from it she was nothing; because she had no other purpose;* because in everything she was, with all her powers, and in every situation in life, she was dedicated to this one vocation; because of all this, she was ever a virgin, ever and always by reason of her divine motherhood as the obedient acceptance of grace."[94] Certain feminist interpretations have surprising resonances with traditional Mariology on this point, seeing Mary as a completely passive figure and thus not a helpful model for women today. Mary Daly famously called Mary the "model rape victim" and argued that Mary's apparent willingness to accept bodily invasion and to mother the son of God is a projected male fantasy.[95] Mary's acceptance of the angel's message in Luke 1, which is not apparently sought or desired, is too quick and does not acknowledge the difficulties she will face.

---

[93] Simone de Beauvoir, *The Second Sex*, trans. H. M. Parshley (New York: Vintage, 1952), 171.

[94] Karl Rahner, *Mary, Mother of the Lord: Theological Meditations*, trans. W. J. O'Hara (New York: Herder and Herder, 1963), 69, emphasis added.

[95] Mary Daly, *Pure Lust: Elemental Feminist Philosophy* (Boston: Beacon, 1984), 102–7, quotation on p. 105. About Daly's insight, Marcella Althaus-Reid says, "Having sex with a woman cannot be taken as a proof of God the Father's heterosexuality, nor should Mary's pregnancy be related to a heterosexual conception of womanhood. As sexual identities emerge amongst relations of subordination and political domination . . . this point is a crucial test of our religious imagination" (*Indecent Theology: Theological Perversions in Sex, Gender and Politics* [New York: Routledge, 2000], 67).

In contrast to positions that emphasize Mary's role as one of an empty space or absolute victim, some feminists emphasize instead her agency in accepting the divine call.[96] This emphasis on agency and autonomy is a key part of feminist work on Mary, as the alternative (that Mary is, indeed, just a vessel) renders her an unusable figure for many contemporary Christian feminists. For example, Rosemary Radford Ruether says, "Luke goes out of his way to stress that Mary's motherhood is a free choice. . . . Luke sees this free choice as an expression of her faith."[97] Likewise, Janice Capel Anderson, in her feminist rhetorical interpretation of the birth narratives, affirms that "Mary's active acceptance of her role is emphasized," especially contrasted with Zechariah, whose incredulity about the divine message serves as a literary foil for Mary's character.[98]

Because unplanned pregnancy and motherhood are key parts of Mary's story, concerns about bodily autonomy, choice, and motherhood thus feature strongly in interpretations of texts about Mary, especially the Annunciation (Luke 1:26–38). The organization Priests for Life, which emphasizes the "strong devotion to the Blessed Mother within the Catholic element of the pro-life movement," connects Mary to unplanned pregnancy in this way:

> Mary faces an unplanned pregnancy. Her response is *Let it be done to me according to your word [Luke 1:38]*. She freely chooses to accept the Child, and in doing so, acknowledges the primacy of the *word*. In other words, the *truth* of God's Word exists before her own choosing. . . . In the pro-life mentality, . . . the *choice* of the mother must *respect the truth of the inherent value of the child*, which does not in any way flow from or depend upon us. *Let it be done to me according to your word*. As we submit to that truth, God

[96] Schaberg, *Illegitimacy of Jesus*, 24.
[97] Rosemary Radford Ruether, *Sexism and God-Talk: Toward a Feminist Theology* (Boston: Beacon, 1983), 153.
[98] Anderson, "Mary's Difference," 191.

does not rob us of our freedom. Instead, He lifts it up to Himself.[99]

As we have seen, the issues of choice and agency have also been at the forefront of feminist scholarship on Mary; even though they are stressing different elements of the story—Mary's role as an active agent versus Mary's decision to accept an unplanned pregnancy—both strands of interpretation hold Mary as an ideal. For example, feminists who emphasize Mary's agency often do so in a way that praises her autonomy and free choice, while simultaneously disparaging submissiveness and self-denial; this parallels the ways in which kyriarchal theology has praised self-sacrifice and humility as paradigmatic virtues for women and as especially incarnated in Mary. That is, there is a desire in both feminist and kyriarchal traditions for Mary to represent an ideal comportment for all women.

One approach that attempts to offer a way out of the impasse in this debate about Mary's agency is found in Cynthia Rigby's essay "Mary and the Artistry of God."[100]Rigby suggests that getting

> caught in the debate about whether Mary had a choice is to risk perceiving her as a secondary player rather than an essential participant in the incarnational event. . . . An alternative approach considers the incarnation as an *essentially* cooperative effort between Mary and God. It is impossible to conceive of the incarnation apart from either God's or Mary's involvement. The Word's self-emptying (*kenosis*) is realized in Mary's God-bearing (*theotokos*) and vice versa; human creativity is included in the creative work of the Creator become creature.[101]

---

[99] Frank Pavone, "The Virgin Mary and Abortion," *Priests for Life*, July 1, 2009, http://www.priestsforlife.org/articles/4537-the-virgin-mary-and-abortion. Father Frank Pavone is the priest who infamously placed the remains of what he claimed was an aborted fetus on the altar while celebrating Mass just days before the November 2016 election, in an effort to encourage congregants to vote for Donald Trump.
[100] In Gaventa and Rigby, *Blessed One*, 145–58.
[101] Ibid., 146.

Even though Rigby's language sometimes emphasizes agency ("Mary bears God in freely acting out of who she is as *theotokos*. To choose against God's coming would be a choice against freedom, a denial of self"[102]), she also uses the metaphor of a dedicated artist who participates in divine work through her craft. Just as an artist does not choose to make art but often feels a sense of compulsion or drive, Rigby argues, Mary partners with God to create—which is not so much a choice as living out a vocation. The feature of the Annunciation that Rigby neglects, however, is the threat that the angel's message presents: The angel invites Mary not to participate in a benign event but in something inherently risky.

Like Rigby's, Jane Schaberg's interpretation attempts to move past some of the dichotomous interpretations of Mary's role in the Annunciation (in other words, Mary is either disciple or victim), but Schaberg does so in a way that acknowledges the potential violence in the narrative. In her 1987 work, *The Illegitimacy of Jesus: A Feminist Theological Interpretation of the Infancy Narratives*, she argues that there is an "almost erased tradition" that lies behind the canonical infancy narratives that Jesus was illegitimately conceived, perhaps as a result of rape.[103] Schaberg argues that "it was the intention—or better, *an* intention—of Matthew and Luke to pass down the tradition they inherited: that Jesus the messiah had been illegitimately conceived during the period when his mother Mary was betrothed to Joseph."[104] By seeing Mary as potentially a victim of rape (though Schaberg acknowledges that Mary could have been seduced or adulterous—I would add that modern and ancient notions of rape, adultery, consent, and seduction are distant enough that we should interrogate what we mean by those terms), but also as one who sings of God's liberation and is chosen to bear a divine child after being (potentially) raped, Schaberg's Mary is both victim and agent—or neither, but something else entirely.[105]

---

[102] Ibid., 154.

[103] Schaberg, *Illegitimacy of Jesus*, 4.

[104] Ibid., 17.

[105] For a discussion of the Lukan Annunciation scene in the context of the "romantic rape tradition," see Betsy Bauman-Martin, "Mary and the Marquise: Reading the Annunciation in the Romantic Rape Tradition," in *Sacred Tropes: Tanakh, New Testament, and Qur'an as Literature and Culture*, ed. Roberta Sterman Sabbath (Boston: Brill, 2009), 217–31.

In short, the scholars surveyed here take varying stances on Mary's characterization. Common feminist concerns include emphasizing Mary's agency and consent in the narratives that feature her, especially ones that focus on her bodily autonomy, yet whether she is portrayed as an active agent or submissive disciple, she is still presented as an ideal individual. The question remains: Is there a way to portray Mary that does not simply idealize her and in so doing make those ideals unattainable? To gain further insight into possible meanings for Mary's story, we turn now to a contemporary instance of maternal activism in which Mary features prominently as simply one mother among many mothers, lamenting her dead child and calling attention to other victims of state violence.

The Maternal Activism of the Madres de Plaza de Mayo

The connections between victimization and agency are especially poignant in the activities of maternal activists. Although a variety of examples could be considered (including COMADRES [Committee of the Mothers and Relatives of the Disappeared, Political Prisoners, and Assassinated of El Salvador], women's groups in Northern Ireland, and various individuals, such as Cindy Sheehan and Jennifer Schumaker[106]), I focus here on the Argentinian *madres de Plaza de Mayo*, because they represent a community that was called into existence amid and in response to violence and political oppression.[107] Moreover, their social critique utilizes notions of sacrifice and self-denial, with explicit reference to Mary, especially related to their roles as mothers.

---

[106] See Janice Nathanson, "Maternal Activism: How Feminist Is It?" in O'Reilly, *Feminist Mothering*, 243–56; Meghan Gibbons, "Political Motherhood in the United States and Argentina," in *Mothers Who Deliver: Feminist Interventions in Public and Interpersonal Discourse*, ed. Jocelyn Fenton Stitt and Pegeen Reichert Powell (Albany: State University of New York Press, 2010), 253–78; and Natalie Wilson, "From Gestation to Delivery: The Embodied Activist Mothering of Cindy Sheehan and Jennifer Schumaker," in Stitt and Powell, *Mothers Who Deliver*, 231–52.

[107] See Meghan Gibbons, "Political Motherhood in the United States and Argentina," in Stitt and Powell, *Mothers Who Deliver*, 253–78; and Bouvard, *Revolutionizing Motherhood*.

From 1977 to 1983, during the "Dirty War" of the Argentinian military junta, government death squads "disappeared" thousands of youths, activists, students, and other "subversives." These *desaparecidos*, or "disappeared ones," were kidnapped, tortured, and killed without trial. Estimates suggest that as many as thirty thousand were disappeared, but the true figures are unknown, as their remains were buried, burned, or dumped in the ocean. To protest this state terrorism, a group of mothers held public demonstrations in front of the presidential mansion, in the plaza where Argentina declared its independence from Spain and where other groups have since claimed their own political rights.[108] Since the war's end, the *madres* have continued to organize on behalf of shared political goals, given their stated concern for all the nation's children.[109]

The *madres* invoked the image of the *Mater Dolorosa*, or Mother of Sorrows, but not one who only passively grieves; the earliest *madres* wore a single carpenter's nail, connecting their plight to Mary's, when they engaged in their weekly protests. One *madre* says they "remember the sacrifice of Christ, nailed to the cross . . . we also have our Christ and we relive the pain of Mary, but we are not even allowed to try to console him with our presence."[110] The *madres* cast themselves in the role of Mary by connecting the suffering of their children, the *desaparecidos*, to Jesus's crucifixion; they are not crucified themselves but are forced to witness the trauma of a child's death. To the traditional images of a suffering Jesus and a witnessing Mary, they add innovative notions of protest and activism. By remembering Mary as a protesting, suffering mother, they also deploy certain powerful aspects of *marianismo*,[111] because "the ultimate expression of *marian-*

---

[108] Bouvard, *Revolutionizing Motherhood*, 1–2.

[109] Elizabeth Borland, "The Mature Resistance of Argentina's *Madres de Plaza de Mayo*," in *Latin American Social Movements: Globalization, Democratization, and Transnational Networks*, ed. Hank Johnston and Paul Almeida (Lanham, MD: Rowman & Littlefield, 2006), 115–30.

[110] Jean-Pierre Bousquet, *Las Locas de La Plaza de Mayo* (Buenos Aires: El Cid Editor, 1983), 47, my translation.

[111] In the words of Rosa M. Gil and Carmen Inoa, "*Marianismo* is about sacred duty, self-sacrifice, and chastity. This cultural phenomenon focuses on dispensing care and pleasure, not receiving them. The *marianismo* mentality fosters an environment in

ismo is the noble sacrifice of self," a notion they utilize to justify their public expressions of grief.[112] According to Meghan Gibbons, "they publicly performed the role of mourning, submissive *mater doloro-sa*."[113] Even though the *madres* distance themselves from explicitly feminist groups and reject the idea that they are reforming gender roles,[114] their mobilization of the image of mourning Mary power-fully suggests that Marian devotion and sacrificial understandings of motherhood are flexible enough to be useful for political change, even while egregious examples of both are being used by oppressive political regimes.

The *madres* are often held up as "the only group that was able to publicly decry the violence of the era without being largely silenced," which most analysts have attributed to the culture of respect toward mothers in a largely Catholic country.[115] Argentinian theologian Marcella Althaus-Reid warns that this version of history risks occlud-ing the *madres'* own suffering for activism:

> The lack of critical insight into the devalued position of motherhood in Latin America has created several ana-lytical mistakes and misjudgements, amongst them the understanding that the Mothers of *Plaza de Mayo* were able to produce a unique movement for the defence of human rights during the dictatorial regime of the 1970s in Argentina, due to the respect that a Marian society pays to mothers. Nothing could be further from the truth. The Mothers of *Plaza de Mayo* have been tortured and killed. . . . They were called *locas* (madwomen, prostitutes). Some of the Mothers remember with irony that they were usually sent to "go and pray to the Virgin Mary" by priests, bishops

---

which women live in the shadows, literally and figuratively, of their men (father, boyfriend, husband, son), children, and family" (quoted in Nora O. Lozano-Diaz, "Ignored Virgin or Unaware Women: A Mexican-American Protestant Reflection on the Virgin of Guadalupe," in Gaventa and Rigby, *Blessed One*, 90).

[112] Ibid., 91.

[113] Gibbons, "Political Motherhood," 264.

[114] Ibid., 271.

[115] Ibid., 254. See also Althaus-Reid, *Indecent Theology*, 51.

and men of power, perhaps with the hope that the Marian worship would domesticate them, make them decent mothers who would educate daughters into decency and not political subversion. Testimonies from tortured victims of the Junta describe how, in the concentration camps, they were forced to pray "Hail Marys" before bedtime.[116]

In their own references to Mary, the *madres* often hold her up as an ideal of maternal strength, devotion, and love—one that they see themselves imitating by protesting state violence—yet their references to Mary strategically emphasize the suffering that they and their children endured, thus indicting the government as the cause of that suffering.[117]

Although the *madres* ostensibly present a traditional image of Mary suffering at her son's crucifixion, the response of clergy and junta officials shows the complexity of the legacy of the Virgin Mary. An army captain criticized their activism, saying, "The Mothers of the *Plaza de Mayo* pervert the role of the mother. . . . I can't imagine the Virgin Mary shouting, protesting, spreading hatred when her son, our God, was snatched from her arms."[118] Though the *madres* insist that their use of Mary is not transgressive, the army captain's response shows how effectively and creatively they deploy certain aspects of Mary's image in order to publicly perform a socially and politically reformed vision of motherhood.

The *madres* organized as an activist community only after their children had been disappeared, tortured, and killed; that is, their public identity as "mothers of the disappeared" is directly tied to a prior experience of violence and trauma. Indeed, they are only publicly visible as a group of maternal activists because of the loss of their children. To speak of "agency" or "choice" in their situation

---

[116] Althaus-Reid, *Indecent Theology*, 51.

[117] Gibbons, "Political Motherhood," 255.

[118] Bouvard, *Revolutionizing Motherhood*, 184; Diana Taylor quotes Monsignore Quarracino (later Archbishop of Buenos Aires) similarly: "I can't imagine the Virgin Mary yelling, protesting and planting the seeds of hate when her son, our Lord, was torn from her hands" (*Disappearing Acts: Spectacles of Gender and Nationalism in Argentina's "Dirty War"* [Durham, NC: Duke University Press, 1997], 196).

resists certain commonplace assumptions about individual autonomy and freedom. Their exercise of agency is in response to an
always already violent world; it is not the unfettered, free choice of
an individual with every option available. Moreover, their agency,
in refusing to collaborate with or ignore state violence but instead
choosing to publicly protest abduction and torture, involves risk and
loss. They endured "dreadful treatment and persistent persecution,"
in the words of the National Commission on the Disappearance
of Persons (CONADEP), suffering "all kinds of threats, aggression,
and even abduction of some of their members, for the sole crime of
asking to see their children come back alive."[119] Their willingness to
risk suffering must be distinguished from deliberate self-harm; their
self-giving is connected to and a direct consequence of their passion
for justice.[120]

Moreover, the maternal activism of the *madres*, while inherently
involving risk and threat, has the benefit of being communal. They
are not known publicly as individual women but collectively as *las
madres*—as a group *and* as mothers.[121] In the wake of violent repres-
sion, their concerns were communal: In their April 1988 newsletter,
the *madres* wrote, "The child of one is the child of all of us, not only
those who are missing, but the ones who are fighting for their rights
today."[122] Thus, as a group, they regard themselves as "permanently
pregnant," gestating a "new generation of political leaders" who
will also be passionate for justice and peace.[123] According to Latin
Americanist Diana Taylor, "they perceived and literally acted out the
difference between motherhood as an individual identity (which for

---

[119] National Commission on the Disappearance of Persons, Nunca Más: *The Report
of the Argentine National Commission on the Disappeared* (New York: Farrar, Straus, and
Giroux, 1986), 422.

[120] See Mercedes, *Power For*, 5.

[121] In addition, certain grandmothers, known as *las abeulas*, also organized and protested the disappearance of their grandchildren (see Rita Arditti, *Searching for Life:
The Grandmothers of the* Plaza de Mayo *and the Disappeared Children of Argentina*
[Berkeley: University of California Press, 1999], and Francisco Goldman, "Children
of the Dirty War," *New Yorker*, March 19, 2012, http://www.newyorker.com/
magazine/2012/03/19/children-of-the-dirty-war).

[122] Quoted in Bouvard, *Revolutionizing Motherhood*, 181.

[123] Ibid., 15.

many of them it was) and motherhood as a collective, political performance that would allow women to protest in the face of a crimi-
nal dictatorship."[124] Their public, collectivist enactment of maternal
activism thus contrasts strongly with individual choices in the private sphere of the home, where sacrificial understandings of motherhood are often located; they are a community of activists exercising
their voices and using their bodies to draw attention to human rights
abuses and to the harm that those abuses bring to all of Argentina's
children.

Contemporary concerns always inform biblical interpretations;
in the case of texts about Mary, modern issues typically center on
women's ordination and leadership, pregnancy (and notions of
choice/agency/inevitability related to pregnancy), and motherhood.
Interpreters often consider these concerns in individualized ways—
that is, focusing on an individual woman and her role, decisions,
and agency. The *madres* present us with a vision of motherhood that
is communally oriented and engaged in struggle, protest, and justice
work. Explicitly foregrounding their experiences and insights allows
us to read texts about Mary with a similar focus: communal instead of
individual, predicated on the prior experience of traumatic violence,
and with an eye toward reforming the maternal role.

Mary and Maternal Self-Sacrifice

Having considered the major interpretive debates about Mary
and sacrificial motherhood, and having seen the ways in which the
experiences of the *madres* can reframe certain interpretative questions,
we now attend to the biblical texts themselves. I do not provide an
exhaustive discussion of each biblical text that mentions Mary but
focus instead on three key texts in the gospels, each of which tends to
earn consideration in interpretations of Mary.[125] As noted above, in

---

[124] Taylor, *Disappearing Acts*, 194.
[125] Although the authors of *Mary in the New Testament* consider all of the texts that reference Mary, they devote the most space to the birth narratives in Matt and Luke, as
well as the crucifixion in John (see Brown et al., *Mary in the New Testament*). Gaventa
considers these three texts, along with the *Protevangelium of James* in *Mary: Glimpses*;
see also her "All Generations Will Call Me Blessed," pp. 47–56, both of which focus

the Lukan infancy narrative, interpreters see Mary in a variety of ways, including a submissive disciple, an active participant in the divine plan, a rape victim, and an agent who chooses her destiny. Two other frequently referenced texts about Mary relate to violence and trauma: Herod's slaughter of the innocents in Matthew's birth narrative, and Jesus entrusting his mother and beloved disciple to one another while he was dying on the cross in John 19. Both of these images fill out the picture of Mary that is mobilized to reflect on motherhood, sacrifice, and devotion. By combining the stories about Mary's unexpected pregnancy, the threat posed to her and her infant child, and her loss of her child on a Roman cross, interpreters weave together disparate stories that create a portrait of Mary as sorrowful, endangered, submissive, and sacrificing mother. Here, I consider these three texts with an eye toward both their violent imperial context and the communal nature of each narrative.

I also emphasize the importance of reading these texts as distinct narratives. Even though interpreters often read all of the canonical texts about Mary as giving information about the "real Mary," this harmonization is often misleading and has potentially grievous consequences.[126] Similar critiques have been made about the scholarly quest for the historical Jesus. As Elisabeth Schüssler Fiorenza argues,

> whether they imagine Jesus as an existentialist religious thinker, a rabbinic teacher, an apocalyptic prophet, a pious Hasid, a revolutionary peasant, a wandering Cynic, a Greco-Roman magician, a healing witch doctor, a nationalist anti-Temple Galilean revolutionary, or a wo/man identified man, the present flood of Historical-Jesus books and articles documents that despite their scientific positivistic rhetoric of facts and historical realism, scholars

---

on these three texts. Cleo McNelly Kearns similarly draws from the birth narratives and the Johannine crucifixion in her *The Virgin Mary, Monotheism, and Sacrifice* (New York: Cambridge University Press, 2008).

[126] For example, see McKnight, *The Real Mary*.

> inescapably fashion the Historical-Jesus in their own image
> and likeness.[127]

Scholarly claims about the historical Mary are similarly diverse and conflicting. Instead of sifting the textual evidence and suggesting a better interpretation of the "real Mary," I hold these three texts together in tension in a way that highlights their distinctiveness and acknowledges the value of multiple canonical (and noncanonical) portraits of Mary. For her theology of Mary, Elizabeth Johnson suggests "crafting a mosaic . . . made up of small fragments of colored stone or marble, called tesserae in the language of art."[128] These tesserae can be fitted into a larger whole, but seeing them as distinct brings to the foreground the interpretive choices that ancient authors made when writing them—and the interpretive choices that modern scholars make when studying them.

Although it seems counterintuitive, I begin with John's crucifixion scene. Certain scholars have argued that "the gospels are written in reverse," that the authors of the gospels and their communities began with the memory of their crucified leader and worked backward from there.[129] Stories about Mary could be approached in the same way. Beginning with John's crucifixion scene allows us to see different things in the infancy narratives: Mary's response to the angel's message, her willingness to parent Jesus, and her surviving Herod's massacre are all assumed for the earliest communities that valued these texts. Instead of asking about her motivations and feelings at the Annunciation as interpreters often do, we could acknowledge that the earliest narratives about Jesus's life (and thus his mother's life) would have, in a way, started at the crucifixion and worked

---

[127] Elisabeth Schüssler Fiorenza, *Jesus and the Politics of Interpretation* (New York: Continuum, 2000), 6.

[128] Johnson, *Truly Our Sister*, 216; see also Johnson, *Dangerous Memories*.

[129] Brown says it is appropriate to speak of the gospels as "developing backward" (see *Birth of the Messiah*, 26). Using Marcus Borg's terminology, the gospels are products of communities that had experienced the "post-Easter Jesus," and the gospels thus contain certain things that are "history metaphorized" (see Marcus J. Borg and N. T. Wright, *The Meaning of Jesus: Two Visions* [San Francisco: HarperSanFrancisco, 1999], 4–8).

backward.[130] Because Jesus was crucified, Jesus must be born, which means that Mary must say yes to the angel's message. The questions of agency, choice, and consent are thus not as pressing; in addition, focusing on the presence of the community in each narrative helps us see that these texts are not just about Mary (or Jesus) but include other figures that allow for a wider vision. In the same way that we witness the *madres*, as a community, engage in social protest for the sake of all their children and have a wider field of vision than their own self or family, we might see Mary as part of narratives that include a whole community and their wellness. Indeed, the *madres* have come to be known publicly as a group in the wake of incredible violence done to their families and communities; in the same way, we know Mary as part of a larger community, after the trauma of the crucifixion. Seeing Mary as a mother-of-martyr instead of a humble, self-sacrificing girl reframes interpretations of all the Marian texts. Knowing that the ending was a given (that is, Jesus was crucified), the author and audience know all along that she will lose her son.[131]

"Stabat Mater": John 19:25–27

The Johannine crucifixion scene, which has inspired countless interpretations, sermons, and artistic renderings, briefly but poignantly evokes the image of a mother watching her son die a gruesome death. Mary is present, even if silent, at the crucifixion in John's gospel, but she is not alone.[132] Most interpreters focus on the meaning of Jesus's words to his mother ("Woman, behold your son") and to his beloved disciple ("Behold your mother") without noting that these are not the only witnesses to the crucifixion in John. At least two other women are also present (maybe three, but

---

[130] Another possible way to begin at "the end" of Mary's story would be to focus on the Acts upper-room scene (Acts 1:13–14), in which Mary is surrounded by others who love Jesus. This is the last time that Mary appears in the Luke–Acts narrative.

[131] Simeon's prophecy in Luke 2:34–35 has the same emphasis; he says to Mary, "This child is destined for the falling and the rising of many in Israel, and to be a sign that will be opposed so that the inner thoughts of many will be revealed—and a sword will pierce your own soul too."

[132] Mary is not in the Synoptic crucifixion texts, though other Marys are named (see Mark 15:40–41 and Matt 27:55–56).

the grammar is unclear): "standing near the cross of Jesus were his mother, and his mother's sister, Mary, the wife of Clopas, and Mary Magdalene" (19:25). Although Jesus addresses only his mother and one disciple, others are there. Focusing on the group of women that witnesses the trauma of the crucifixion highlights not only the violence of an imperial system attempting to terrorize and fragment a community but also the subversive presence of that community that resists dispersion.[133] Mary and others may risk retaliation by being present at Golgatha, yet their willingness to persist as a community is a powerful witness to imperial weaknesses. Moreover, in the same way that the *madres'* protests involved bodily presence and absence (that is, the absence of their children's bodies and the presence of their own bodies in the Plaza de Mayo), the presence of women at the cross in John 19 (and the presence of other women at the tomb) is a vision of communal care for particular bodies in the midst of pain.[134]

Pain and loss are key features of nearly every interpretation of Marian texts; even explanations of the Immaculate Conception, which emphasize that Mary was "exempt from human passions, preserved from temptations, especially those of a sexual nature, immune from wrestling with issues, spared ambiguity when it came to decisions, always in full possession of her wits, clearly knowing God's plan for herself and her son and more than willing to carry it out," will still allow that she felt great sorrow at the cross—"but even here, it is said, she willingly sacrificed her son for the redemption of the world."[135] In the words of *Lumen Gentium*, Mary was present at the cross, "grieving exceedingly with her only begotten Son, uniting herself with a maternal heart with His sacrifice, and

---

[133] Jean Kim discusses the use of crucifixion as a terrorizing mechanism on p. 203 of *Woman and Nation: An Intercontextual Reading of the Gospel of John from a Postcolonial Feminist Perspective* (Boston: Brill, 2004). For an exploration of similar themes in the context of Q 7:31–35 and 11:14–20, see Melanie Johnson-DeBaufre, "Communities Resisting Fragmentation: Q and the Work of James C. Scott," in *Oral Performance, Popular Tradition, and Hidden Transcript in Q*, ed. Richard A. Horsley, Semeia Studies 60 (Atlanta: Society of Biblical Literature, 2006), 193–207.

[134] For a discussion of the ways in which women nationalists are often viewed as less threatening than their male counterparts, see Kim, *Woman and Nation*, 204–6.

[135] Johnson, *Truly Our Sister*, 108.

lovingly consenting to the immolation of this Victim which she herself had brought forth."[136]

The image of Mary at the crucifixion, a mother watching her son be executed by the state, is one that has real poignancy for women, like the *madres*, who have witnessed and experienced such tragedies. Johnson compares Mary to other mourning Jewish mothers (during the Roman era, Christian Crusades, Russian pogroms, and Nazi Holocaust), other mourning Asian and Latin American women whose children are massacred and imprisoned for justice work, and other women who are galvanized to "non-violent action to stop the violence as the only appropriate expression of faith."[137] This passage has provided resources for reflection for liberation theologians focused on the need for a "defiant energy to refuse evil and work for a transformed world."[138] For example, theologian Itumeleng Mosala shows how the image of Mary with her dying son has had powerful effects for black audiences in South Africa: "When black preachers expound on this text [John 19:25–27], they invariably raise issues that bring tears to the eyes of the so-called illegitimate sons and daughters and their unmarried mothers. A great deal of weeping and sorrow cover the congregations at this point. It is important, however, to realize that the sadness expressed at this time . . . is over the economic disinvestment imposed on a single-parent family by the death of a son or a daughter."[139] The "Stabat Mater" image evokes different themes for liberationist interpreters than for more traditional interpreters: rather than "willingly consenting" to her son's death, here she mourns structural violence.

Instead of focusing exclusively on Mary and her unique sacrifice, interpreters could foreground the presence of a devoted community witnessing the execution of one of their own. According to John

---

[136] Second Vatican Council, *Lumen Gentium* [Dogmatic Constitution on the Church], Vatican Website, November 21, 1964, sec. 58, http://www.vatican.va/archive/hist_councils/ii_vatican_council /documents/vat-ii_const_19641121_lumen-gentium_en.html.
[137] Johnson, *Truly Our Sister*, 297.
[138] Ann Loades, "Mary: Bone of Contention," in *From the Margins 2: Women of the New Testament and Their Afterlives*, ed. Christine E. Joynes and Christopher Rowland (Sheffield, England: Sheffield Phoenix, 2009), 58.
[139] Itumeleng J. Mosala, *Biblical Hermeneutics and Black Theology in South Africa* (Grand Rapids, MI: Eerdmans, 1989), 187.

19:25–26, the people who see the crucifixion are Jesus's mother, his aunt, and some close friends (Mary Magdalene and the anonymous "beloved disciple"[140]); it is not, then, an intimate moment between mother and son, even though the artistic tradition stemming from this text might suggest such a scene. Expanding our field of vision to include the presence of a wider community allows biblical interpreters to emphasize the violence of imperial systems and the power of presence amid communal trauma. If Mary is not alone at the crucifixion but is one of many women who experience loss and yet remain present, this presents an alternate vision of motherhood. Rather than prescribing maternity as simplistically and harmfully connected to suffering, sacrifice, and pain, motherhood is here connected to communal solidarity and care as a response to violent loss. Like the *madres*, then, Mary and her companions refuse to turn away from the victims of state violence.

Rachel Weeping for Her Children: Matthew 1–2

When Joseph plans to "dismiss [Mary] quietly" (Matt 1:19), an angel appears in his dream and tells him not to fear taking Mary as his wife (1:20). Joseph obeys the angel (as he does later in 2:14 and 2:21). If Joseph, like Mary, faces difficult decisions mediated through a divine messenger, chooses ultimately in favor of parenting a holy child, and perseveres in spite of the (presumed) stigma around the child's illegitimacy, why do interpretations of Luke's Mary emphasize her agency, choice, and discipleship while interpretations of Matthew's Joseph do not? Do we assume that concerns about pregnancy, childbearing, marriage, and consent are women's concerns? Is it because Mary was apparently consenting to pregnancy while Joseph was consenting to marry a woman who was already pregnant?

It would be possible to focus on the ways in which Joseph is portrayed as an agent who freely chooses to father Jesus with Mary

---

[140] A minority of interpreters have suggested ways that the Beloved Disciple could be identified as Mary Magdalene; for some of the problems with this view, see Jane Schaberg, *The Resurrection of Mary Magdalene: Legends, Apocrypha, and the Christian Testament* (New York: Continuum, 2004), 344–45.

(just as interpreters of Luke 1–2 emphasize that Mary freely chooses to mother Jesus). This focus on Joseph would have the benefit of including both Mary *and* Joseph in the larger communal vision that I am suggesting here, but emphasizing Joseph's agency could simply replicate the interpretive trajectory of scholarship on Luke's infancy narrative, by applying similar insights to Joseph instead of Mary. If we instead place Mary and Joseph in a larger community, it becomes clear that they face violence and threat directed at themselves, their child, and the town. Because the narrative has a communal focus, discussing the birth of Jesus amid communal violence, political intrigue, and imperial rule allows for us to see Mary differently in this text.[141]

Schaberg's emphasis on the overtones of sexual violence in this text highlights the multiple possible interpretations of how Mary became pregnant. There is no Annunciation to her in Matthew, so the narrative begins with an already-pregnant Mary; the possibility that sexual violence caused her pregnancy is just one example of the violent threats faced by their family and community. Mary is just one among many mothers who experiences violence and loss in Matthew's infancy narrative; the genealogy references four other women whose stories involve loss or threat, and even more poignantly, Herod's massacre of all the baby boys around Bethlehem (2:16) inspires the inclusion of Jeremiah's prophecy: "A voice was heard in Ramah, wailing and loud lamentation, Rachel weeping for her children; she refused to be consoled, because they are no more" (Matt. 2:18; Jer. 31:15).[142]

In line with methods of biblical interpretation that highlight the ethical accountability of the interpreter, Gary Phillips has argued for such an interpretation of this pericope in which violence is inflicted on so many innocents.[143] About the "advent spectacle," he

---

[141] Although it was not yet published when my manuscript went to press, my argument here resonates with Christopher Frilingos's work on infancy gospels, which he says should be more rightly called family gospels. See his *Jesus, Mary, and Joseph: Culture and Christianity in Ancient Family Gospels* (Philadelphia: University of Pennsylvania Press, 2017).

[142] Gaventa, "All Generations Will Call Me Blessed," 125.

[143] See an initial discussion of the ways in which interpreters engage ethical concerns above in "Approaching Maternal Self-Sacrifice as a Flexible Discourse" in the introduction to this book.

says, an "understated but central aspect . . . is the violence inflicted upon children. The wholesale violence announces the arrival and survival of Jesus, for within Matthew's careful[ly] constructed narrative plot the unnamed children are the necessary collateral damage that leads to Jesus's eventual passion and the subsequent birth of Christianity."[144] Phillips persuasively argues that biblical critics must "interrupt the violence and protect . . . the innocents"; elsewhere, he has warned that readers of the Bible who do not consciously adopt an ethical stance may risk "contribut[ing] to the formation of a culture that makes the murder of the innocents natural and inevitable."[145] Although Phillips's focus in this discussion is reading violent gospel narratives in a post-Shoah world,[146] his plea for biblical scholars to be better interpreters of violent biblical texts and, equally important, "better analysts and interpreters of their contemporary culture, attentive to the ways in which the biblical narrative is foundational to lived experience for better or worse"[147] is also relevant to my focus on sacrificial understandings of motherhood. In the same way that biblical scholars should acknowledge the many ways that the text about the massacre of the innocents has played out genocidally in subsequent history, they can also highlight the violence done to mothers and families in the wake of such destructive and powerful biblical texts.

---

[144] Gary A. Phillips, "More Than the Jews . . . His Blood Be upon All the Children: Biblical Violence, Genocide, and Responsible Reading," in *Confronting Genocide: Judaism, Christianity, Islam*, ed. Steven L. Jacobs (Lanham, MD: Lexington Books, 2009), 84.

[145] Quotations ibid., 80, and Gary A. Phillips, "The Killing Fields of Matthew's Gospel," in *A Shadow of Glory: Reading the New Testament after the Holocaust*, ed. Tod Linafelt (New York: Routledge, 2002), 237.

[146] I use *Shoah* instead of the more familiar *Holocaust*. About this distinction, Tod Linafelt writes, "Many have objected to the term [that is, Holocaust, which means a whole burnt offering sacrificed to God] being applied, given its religious and sacrificial overtones, to the murder of six million Jews, and one often finds the term Shoah (Hebrew for 'destruction') substituted instead" ("Introduction," in *A Shadow of Glory: Reading the New Testament after the Holocaust*, ed. Tod Linafelt [New York: Routledge, 2002], x).

[147] Phillips, "Killing Fields," 235.

A Sword Will Pierce Your Own Soul: Luke 1–2

Luke's infancy narrative could also be understood as a narrative of a community rather than of a single important woman. As many interpreters have noted, Luke's gospel begins not with Mary but with Zechariah and Elizabeth, parents of John the Baptist.[148] Indeed, Mary is mentioned for the first time in 1:27, and the transition to her portion of the narrative is marked by the words "in the sixth month"—that is, the sixth month of Elizabeth's unlikely pregnancy. Interpreters commonly note a "stair-step" pattern here: whatever happens to Elizabeth is replicated and surpassed by what happens to Mary. Elizabeth and Zechariah are an elderly couple for whom conception is unlikely; Mary is a virgin (παρθενος, 1:27), for whom conception should be impossible (compare with Mary's question in 1:34). Elizabeth's son will be "great in the sight of the Lord" (1:15), while Mary's son will be "great, and will be called son of the most high" (1:32). This oscillation between Elizabeth and Mary allows interpreters to demonstrate the uniqueness of Mary and Jesus, especially when compared with the miracle of John's birth to Elizabeth. Rather than being foils *for* the holy family, Zechariah and Elizabeth could simply be seen as *part of* the family. Seeing the ways in which the text has a communal orientation allows us to reframe issues of individual autonomy and personal agency as issues of community wellness.

The presence of the community is also apparent in other textual moments. After Elizabeth bears a son, "her neighbors and relatives . . . rejoice . . . with her" (1:58) and come to celebrate his ritual circumcision on the eighth day. The members of the community plan to name the child after his father, Zechariah, but Elizabeth insists that the child should be called John (in accordance with the angel's directive to Zechariah in 1:13). When Zechariah confirms the name, the reaction of the community is a focus: "Fear came over all their

---

[148] Stephanie Buckhanon Crowder's new book was released too close to my own book deadlines for me to fully incorporate her insightful readings of biblical mothers, including Mary. Interested readers should consult *When Momma Speaks: The Bible and Motherhood from a Womanist Perspective* (Louisville, KY: Westminster John Knox, 2016).

neighbors, and all these things were talked about throughout the entire hill country of Judea. All who heard them pondered them" (1:65–66). The imperial census likewise has a communal, or rather global, horizon: The emperor orders "all the world" (πᾶσαν τὴν οἰκουμένην) to be registered in 2:1.

Mosaic Mary

Instead of seeing Mary as a paradigmatic example of choice and agency, feminist interpreters could show that readers join Mary's story *in media res* and that her response to a difficult situation is what is most useful for women. In the same way that the *madres* in Argentina have not chosen a personal and political crisis but rather have responded to incredible loss with creativity, indignation, and resolve, Mary's agency could be reframed: her response to the Annunciation is a given, so she is already involved (in a way, already pregnant and her story will move forward inevitably, like a pregnancy) and her agency is thus in her participation.[149] This would not idealize Mary but would acknowledge the complexity of the various gospel narratives, differentiate the ways in which interpreters have used and appropriated Mary, and highlight the resources her story/stories present to suffering women.

In a discussion of papal pronouncements on gender roles, Judith Butler argues for the importance of questions, conflicts, and discussion:

> If there is a social site in which sexuality is imbued with paralyzing judgments, it is doubtless in and through the papal pulpit. And, because it is a site of power, it must be engaged critically and insistently until open and sustained conflict on the place and meaning of religious authority of this kind yields hope for intimate associations and

---

[149] In certain ways, this evokes themes from mariological reflection on the title *Theotokos*. Many interpretations of the doctrine of the *Theotokos* will emphasize that Mary's response is already known because she has always been the *Theotokos*. See Sarah Jane Boss, "The Title Theotokos," in Boss, *Mary*, 50–55.

gendered practices that have not always been accorded "dignity" within society. Let a thousand conflicts of interpretation bloom, I say! And I say this not because pluralism alone will ease our minds but because the proliferation of possible interpretations may well lead to the subversion of an authority that grounds itself in what may not be questioned. In such a world, questions, loud and clear, remain intrinsic goods.[150]

Interpretations of Mary as a self-sacrificing mother are a different "site of power" than the one Butler is discussing but are still "imbued with paralyzing judgments"; whether or not they originate from the papal pulpit, these interpretations often idealize the "real" Mary and a monolithic understanding of motherhood as submissive. Allowing, or even demanding, "a thousand conflicts of interpretation" about biblical texts that include Mary would thus subvert the interpretive stances that ground themselves "in what may not be questioned." Moreover, the various conflicts of interpretation also highlight the flexibility of maternal self-sacrifice as neither natural nor normal but strategic. By holding these conflicts of interpretation, both ancient and modern, together like the tesserae in a mosaic, we are able to acknowledge the diverse effects of these interpretations for mothers in particular and women's lives in general. Highlighting the ways in which women such as the *madres* use Marian imagery and notions of maternal self-sacrifice in struggles for justice indicates that not all interpretive conflicts are necessarily problems to be resolved in favor of a single "better" interpretation. Instead, the ethical results of various interpretive choices can be the basis for adjudicating among interpretations.[151]

---

[150] Judith Butler, "Afterword," in *Bodily Citations: Religion and Judith Butler*, ed. Ellen T. Armour and Susan M. St. Ville (New York: Columbia University Press, 2006), 276.
[151] See Johnson-DeBaufre, "Communities Resisting Fragmentation," 206–7, where she says, "I propose these interpretations, therefore, not only because they are historically plausible and textually defensible, but also because they are ethically preferable. . . . The disciplines of the academy often do not encourage such self-critical reflexivity among scholars."

CHAPTER 2

Spectacular Mothers: The Sun Woman and Other Mothers in Revelation

The Book of Revelation has four female figures, whose characteristics, actions, and titles make this text a fruitful place to illustrate some of the various uses of maternal imagery in a narrative context of social violence. In and through these figures, John and his communities struggle to define themselves over and against the larger Greco-Roman world and other Judeo-Christian groups that likely had much in common with the audience of Revelation. By focusing on each female figure in turn, I show the ways in which these discourses of violence and sacrifice are tied closely to notions of motherhood, especially as communities wrestle with questions of time and tradition, suffering and loss, and community relationships (both intragroup and intergroup). I consider how this text presents motherhood as both a threatened and threatening subjectivity; the Sun Woman (or Woman Clothed with the Sun), for example, endures the loss of her child amid a heavenly war (Rev. 12:1–17). Two other maternal figures—Jezebel (2:20–25) and Babylon (17:1–18:24)—receive violent punishment from heaven. Last, the Heavenly Jerusalem, figured as a chaste bride, is distanced from the pain and complexity of motherhood. Here, I read Revelation's maternal figures alongside narratives from mothers who were combatants in the civil war in El Salvador during the 1980s and 1990s. Women fought on the side of the guerrillas (the Farabundo Martí National Liberation Front, or FMLN) from the beginning of the Salvadoran civil war and often provided other forms of support for the FMLN at great personal risk. These mothers' varying testimonials, stories of both strength and hope, on the one hand, and extreme pain, on the other, invite us to a greater appreciation of the extreme forms of maternal pain and violence evoked in Revelation, written within a context of imperial occupation and imbued with images of holy war.

Especially when interpreters focus on gender in Revelation and/ or on these female figures in particular, violence is often a crucial issue. After looking at the ways in which Revelation genders the violence of holy war, I turn to the experiences of women in the FMLN, to highlight the complexities of women's choices in a violent context. I then return to a close examination of each female figure in Revelation, beginning with the Woman Clothed with the Sun in Revelation 12. Her story is the most detailed and is located as a crucial moment in the narrative; moreover, she is often connected to Mary, considered in the previous chapter. Finally, I focus on the other female figures who are symbolically or potentially connected to motherhood: Jezebel, whose children are struck dead; Babylon the great, "mother of whores"; and the Heavenly New Jerusalem, who is adorned as a bride.

Gender, Violence, and Apocalypse

Many feminist interpreters see the depictions of the four female figures in Revelation as evidence that this text is threatening to women; Tina Pippin writes, "The Bride is made into *polis*, city, the Whore gang raped and burned and eaten, the Woman Clothed with the Sun is a reproductive vessel who is exiled subsequent to giving birth, and Jezebel is destroyed."[152] Virginia Burrus, however, has shown that Revelation is full of ambiguity and ambivalence, even as Babylon's "performance anticipates the arrival of a sharply contrasting female figure, the chaste bride Jerusalem, establishing an opposition between harlot and virgin—between worldly and heavenly cities—that would seem calculated to dispel ambivalence. (We know exactly which woman we *ought* to prefer.)"[153] This same ten-

---

[152] Tina Pippin, *Apocalyptic Bodies: The Biblical End of the World in Text and Image* (New York: Routledge, 1999), 119.

[153] Virginia Burrus, *Saving Shame: Martyrs, Saints, and Other Abject Subjects* (Philadelphia: University of Pennsylvania Press, 2008), 16–17.

sion is apparent when considering these female figures in relation to their mothering: The audience could easily see Jezebel and Babylon as "bad mothers" and the Sun Woman as a "good mother," with Jerusalem, the chaste bride prepared for her divine spouse, also having potential to be a good mother. In fact, this dichotomy is set up in the text and is the expected interpretation. But these multiple images of motherhood that involve loss, threat, protection, and reproduction also allow us to see the ways these figures are being used in larger discourses about communal identity formation, continuity, and suffering. The female figures are therefore far more similar than we expect them to be, disrupting our expectation that John's vision has only sharp, dualistic oppositions. That is, although "we know exactly which woman we *ought* to prefer," we can instead consider the ways in which these diverse images of motherhood, childhood, violence, and sacrifice are flexible and productive for John and his subsequent interpreters.

One of the most pervasive themes in Revelation is the violent punishment of God's enemies. Perhaps, as Stephen D. Moore suggests, Revelation itself is all about war. Moore writes, "Revelation can plausibly be said to be about the establishment of God's kingdom on earth. How is this kingdom to be established? Through the messianic war. And what is the messianic war? An activity that, on the symbolic level, is conducted exclusively by male subjects . . . and is constitutive of the masculinity of those subjects, since it is ultimately directed against the feminine."[154] This focus on violence and war leads interpreters like Pippin to ask if "this violent version of the end of time [is] the story women want to tell."[155] Her warning is appropriate, especially since a violent apocalypse may limit our capacity for creativity in our approach to social change. But Pippin also argues that interpreters must respond to Revelation by acknowledging the "apocalypse of women"—the root of gender

---

[154] Stephen D. Moore, *God's Beauty Parlor: And Other Queer Spaces in and around the Bible* (Stanford, CA: Stanford University Press, 2001), 186.

[155] Tina Pippin, "The Revelation to John," in *Searching the Scriptures*, Vol. 2: *A Feminist Commentary*, ed. Elisabeth Schüssler Fiorenza (New York: Crossroad, 1994), 123.

relations, which destroys women as women.[156] In order to read Revelation with the apocalypse of women in mind, Pippin says, we should listen "to the voices of women past and present who speak out of their own apocalypses, their own crises and visions of the future."[157] Avoiding Revelation or rejecting it as hopelessly misogynistic risks ignoring the violent realities that many women face; for this reason, I propose reading Revelation's female figures alongside the stories of women combatants in El Salvador. Facing their own "apocalypses," these women highlight the complexity of motherhood in violent contexts.

Considering the connections between motherhood and violence (in both ancient and modern textual and sociopolitical contexts) should complicate our assumptions about what a "good" mother is and whether mothers should have to be self-sacrificing. Moreover, we can problematize the idea that self-sacrifice is what mothers "naturally" do. The particular experience of childbirth, usually understood as involving meaningful, natural, productive pain, is perhaps the place where this link is made most clearly. Thus, we may ask, are maternal experiences, including childbirth, still understood as purposeful suffering in violent contexts?

The Apocalypse of Women: Self-Sacrificial Rhetoric as Resistance

Before and during the Salvadoran civil war of the 1980s and 1990s, ordinary citizens suffered at the hands of their own government; "union leaders, *campesinos*, teachers, churchworkers and others 'were disappeared' by government death squads."[158] Many women fought on the side of the guerrillas and provided other forms of support for the FMLN, at great personal risk, and yet the cultural expectation for these women was still strongly oriented around motherhood. Psychologist Ana Cristina Ibáñez interviewed former combatants about their experiences during

---

[156] Ibid., 110.
[157] Ibid.
[158] Scott Wright, ed., *El Salvador: A Spring Whose Waters Never Run Dry* (Washington, DC: Epica Task Force, 1990), 11.

the war and describes the value placed on motherhood in traditional Salvadoran culture: "A woman could be forgiven anything except not bearing children."[159] Given this cultural expectation, plus the circumstances of the war, women often found themselves in a classic double bind: They were expected to bear children and yet having children as FMLN guerrillas could endanger not only the children but also the mothers and their comrades. Testimonials indicate that mothers sometimes killed their babies rather than risk the government death squads hearing the babies' cries. "Bringing children into the world under circumstances of war, in the hope of offering them a better future, and then being obliged to sacrifice them in the name of that same future, created a schizophrenic, cruel situation that women could not resolve," Ibáñez explains.[160]

These Salvadoran women did not describe a world in which they freely and dispassionately chose whatever action seemed appropriate; rather, they portrayed their actions against the backdrop of impossible choices and incredible suffering. Nadia and her husband were both FMLN combatants, so their fourteen-month-old son lived with Nadia's parents while she and her husband fought. It was difficult for them to leave their son, especially at such a young age, but Nadia said,

> Under the war conditions and system imposed on our country, I don't feel my concern as a mother is restricted simply to one child, there are millions of children in the country. I even believe that I wouldn't have the moral qualifications to educate my son with, if I weren't directly taking part in my people's liberation. It's an act of hypocrisy to collaborate in the way things are in the country. It's a contradiction, but one has to see how to resolve it. The interests of the whole population take first place, they're what have

---

[159] Ana Cristina Ibáñez, "El Salvador: War and Untold Stories: Women Guerrillas," in *Victims, Perpetrators, or Actors?: Gender, Armed Conflict, and Political Violence*, ed. Caroline O. N. Moser and Fiona C. Clark (New York: Zed, 2001), 120.
[160] Ibid., 122.

to prevail over all our personal activities. For me, the costs
came high in learning this because of the pain it entailed,
but I'm fully convinced that motherhood has a not merely
personal but also an historical dimension.[161]

Nadia's insight that she would not be morally qualified to mother
her own child if she collaborated with the status quo challenges an
atomized view of motherhood concerned solely with one's own biological children. Although she acknowledged the potential contradiction, she still claimed that involvement in this liberation movement
was a way of parenting. For Nadia, involvement in the war was an
opportunity to demonstrate concern for the entire nation's children
instead of only her own biological child.

Another mother who fought with the guerrillas, Karla, affirmed
a similar concern for other people's children; she wrote, "It was very,
very hard to leave [my son with my mother while I went to the mountains to fight]. I cried. But I knew what I did was for my baby, and
not only for him, but for everybody, because for me everybody is my
son."[162] Likewise, Marina, who worked for a trade union and collaborated with the guerrillas, concluded a description of her involvement
in the civil war this way: "I'm in struggle so that my children won't
have to be, or if they do it'll be in defence of what we've handed on
to them."[163] These mothers, like the madres de Plaza de Mayo, have
an expanded vision of motherhood that cannot include only one's
own children but necessarily includes other people's children and,
indeed, the whole nation and its future. Thus, leaving behind their
own children to fight with the guerrillas was not incongruous with
their understanding of maternity but was rather an extension of it.

A Salvadoran guerilla named Marta was captured by the national
guard when she was nine months pregnant; her testimony about the

---

[161] Claribel Alegria, They Won't Take Me Alive: Salvadorean Women in Struggle for
National Liberation, trans. Amanda Hopkinson (London: Women's Press, 1983), 109.
[162] Karla Ramirez, "El Salvador," in Her War Story: Twentieth-Century Women Write
about War, ed. Sayre P. Sheldon (Carbondale: Southern Illinois University Press,
1999), 312.
[163] Alegria, They Won't Take Me Alive, 127.

torture she endured and the circumstances of her son's birth contains its own dragons and enemies (compare with Rev. 12:3):

> They beat me. When they seized us, they threw us face down onto the floor. Then, when they blindfolded us and bundled us into the truck, I began to yell . . . so that the news should spread through our district and shouted my mum's phone number. . . . They forced each of us into separate cells. They threw me in one too, then went down the line hitting us. They beat my back with a rifle butt. I started going into labour, but didn't say anything about it to them. They had me stretched out on a bed and I couldn't stand the labour pains any longer. . . . Then they noticed that I was in pain and ordered me to start "singing." I told them that I didn't know anything. They kept on trying to make me talk.[164]

Eventually, Marta was taken to a hospital, and through the hospital staff's cunning clandestine work, she gave birth, remained in the hospital for a week with her baby, and safely snuck out unnoticed.

Narratives like these can help us reframe certain feminist conversations about the harmfulness of maternal self-sacrifice. Consider, for example, Pippin's observation about martyrdom and Revelation: "Martyrdom becomes another form of patriarchal abuse. Christ is more than a sacrificial lamb who resurrected into a mythic warrior hero. Women have to refuse the call to mimic such sacrifice."[165] Although Pippin's point may be compelling in certain contexts, the narratives about women FMLN combatants show how the brutal nature of war affects women and their children. Though they did experience great suffering for a larger cause, women who fought with the FMLN do not describe themselves as sacrificial lambs but instead highlight the complexity of their choices under a brutal regime and their hope for a better future. Their narratives also

---

[164] Ibid., 84.
[165] Pippin, "Revelation to John," 125.

demonstrate the rhetorical power of using the mother-child bond to highlight suffering; what could evoke more pathos than the image of a woman giving birth under torture or a mother being separated from her child? Rejecting the connection between motherhood and martyrdom out of hand risks occluding these experiences and flattening the complex political and ethical work that these mothers' narratives perform.

Pathos and Fear in the Vision of the Sun Woman

Revelation 12 opens with the story of an unnamed woman in labor, hunted by a dragon who is waiting to devour her newborn son.[166] She is introduced as an astronomically powerful feminine figure, a "great portent . . . clothed with the sun, with the moon under her feet, and on her head a crown of twelve stars" (12:1). As she is giving birth, another portent appears: "a great red dragon, with seven heads and ten horns, and seven diadems on his heads" (12:3). Although the dragon stands threateningly close while she births her son, her child is protected when he is "snatched away" and the woman flees to the wilderness (12:5). At this point, John describes a war in heaven between Michael and his angels and the dragon and his angels. When the dragon is defeated, he is thrown back down to earth and continues to pursue (ἐδίωξεν) the woman (12:13). First, she flies away from the dragon on "the two wings of the great eagle" (12:14); then, when the dragon tries to drown her in a flood, Earth swallows the flood and saves her (12:16). Although the woman is not mentioned after 12:16, the dragon remains "angry with the woman" and continues to "make war on the rest of her children [τῶν λοιπῶν τοῦ σπέρματος αὐτῆς], those who keep the commandments of God and hold the testimony [μαρτυρίαν] of Jesus" (12:17).

---

[166] Although the woman is unnamed, the dragon is identified twice; see Rev 12:9 ("the great dragon was thrown down, that ancient serpent, who is called the Devil and Satan, the deceiver of the whole world") and Rev 20:2 ("He seized the dragon, that ancient serpent, who is the Devil and Satan, and bound him for a thousand years"). See David E. Aune, *Revelation 6–16*, Word Biblical Commentary 52B (Nashville, TN: Thomas Nelson, 1998), 680.

Exegetes have long attempted to assign an identity to this power-ful woman and have suggested numerous options; she has variously been identified with the Virgin Mary/Our Lady of Guadalupe, Israel, the Church, the Heavenly Jerusalem, the persecuted people of God, a constellation, Isis, the Queen of Heaven, Eve, and, more recently, a Goddess.[167] Immediately after her cosmic entrance, labor begins, and she bellows, "tormented" or "tortured" (βασανιζομένη) by the birth-ing process. Pippin focuses on this scene when discussing women's silence in Revelation ("We hear her anguish but not her words."[168]); however, the word used in 12:2 for her crying out (κράζει) can also describe the "urgent speech of a prophet."[169] This woman's act of bringing forth new life is thus not necessarily portrayed as passive suffering but as strong and, indeed, prophetic.

Though the woman is tortured by birth pangs, this pain (like the labor pangs of creation in Rom. 8:22) is productive and purposeful, as it is linked to the hope of new life. Like Jezebel of Thyatira (whom I consider below), the Woman Clothed with the Sun and her son are caught up in violent surroundings, as she gives birth in the presence of a devouring dragon and amid heavenly war (12:7–12). Her son, nearly eaten at the moment of his birth, is the one who "will rule all of the nations with a rod of iron" (12:5; cf. 19:15). Even though he is born into such threat and turmoil, however, there is hope for his survival, and his mother is later saved by Earth, the great eagle, and the desert: "The woman was given the two wings of the great eagle, so that she could fly from the serpent into the wilderness, to her place where she is nourished. . . . Then from his mouth the serpent poured water like a river after the water, to sweep her away with the flood. But the earth came to the help of the woman; it opened its mouth and swallowed the river that the dragon had poured from his mouth"

---

[167] Catherine Keller, *Apocalypse Now and Then: A Feminist Guide to the End of the World* (Boston: Beacon, 1996), 64–66; Pippin, "Revelation to John," 118; and Aune, *Revelation 6–16*, 680.

[168] Tina Pippin, "The Heroine and the Whore: The Apocalypse of John in Feminist Perspective," in *From Every People and Nation: The Book of Revelation in Intercultural Perspective*, ed. David M. Rhoads (Minneapolis, MN: Fortress, 2005), 137.

[169] Walter Bauer, William F. Arndt, and F. Wilbur Gingrich, *A Greek-English Lexicon of the New Testament and Other Early Christian Literature*, ed. Frederick W. Danker (Chicago: University of Chicago Press, 2000), 564.

(12:14–16). These personified natural elements show solidarity with the woman and provide her nourishment and safety.

She is "nursed" (τρέφωσιν, 12:6, 12:14; usually translated "nourished" or "fed") in the wilderness. The pain of childbirth and threat of the dragon are not fatal or final; indeed, after she and her son are safe, the dragon "went off to make war on the rest of her children, those who keep the commandments of God and hold the testimony [μαρτυρίαν] of Jesus" (12:17). The Sun Woman and her son, like the rest of her children, are protected amid danger and survive serious threats, including childbirth, war, and a ravenous dragon.

Using a threatened maternal figure, John constructs an identity for Christ followers that links productive pain with hope for the future—indeed, hope for the future that includes the final annihilation of God's enemies. John also works to produce a tradition that does not remain centered on this maternal figure. The Sun Woman's role as a mother in the narrative ends with her labor. Interpreters are conflicted about the significance of this abrupt ending. One the one hand, Pippin emphasizes that it signifies a lack of interest in the Sun Woman's maternal contribution: "After her reproductive activity is completed, she is no longer useful; and so she ends up in the wilderness. The traditional female values that customarily accompany the act of mothering—nurturing and caretaking—are suppressed."[170] Her son is apparently nurtured in heaven apart from her efforts. In this reading, the Sun Woman guarantees continuity and tradition but seems to do so in a way that actively erases her. On the other hand, instead of seeing the Sun Woman here as "subdued, tamed, and under control," as Pippin does, we could emphasize instead the hope for the future that this scene contains.[171] Though her role in the story is brief, the Sun Woman's labor is a turning point in Revelation. As Catherine Keller says, "The Sun Woman's labor is the book's first *glimpse* of hope; heretofore hope has been merely *voiced*."[172] In a movement that resonates with Marta's traumatic but ultimately hopeful birthing experience in war-torn El Salvador, the Sun Woman's agonizing labor

---

[170] Pippin, "The Heroine and the Whore," 136.
[171] Ibid.
[172] Keller, *Apocalypse Now and Then*, 66.

and birth create an ambivalently promising scene amid a disturbing vision of the future.

After the heavenly war, the dragon first pursues the Sun Woman and then moves on to attack the rest of her children (12:13–17). Verse 16—in which a personified Earth comes to the woman's aid by swallowing the river that the dragon has poured from its mouth—is typically read as a happy ending for this woman, but this is a questionable reading. To be sure, Earth and other natural elements save the Sun Woman from the dragon, so perhaps she herself is safe, but her other children are not safe, as is made clear by the attack on them in 12:17: "The dragon was angry with the woman, and went off to make war on the rest of her children." It might seem that the heavenly war in verses 7–12 interrupts the Sun Woman's narrative, but the war and its aftermath are actually a key part of the Sun Woman's story; indeed, her son, conscripted into the divine army, will later "rule all the nations with a rod of iron" (12:5). In this way, John uses the Sun Woman to construct an identity for the audience (that is, they are the ones who "keep the commandments and hold the testimony of Jesus") as threatened, because they are in relationship with the Sun Woman.

The Sun Woman and her children, including her conscripted son, are visible in the narrative only as victims of war. As the experience of the Salvadoran civil war is integral to the experience of the women of FLMN, so the Sun Woman's story is embedded in a larger story of cosmic war. We would not know the experiences of the women in the FMLN without the existence of the Salvadoran civil war; likewise, we cannot know the Sun Woman's narrative apart from this vision of heavenly war. This statement is not to justify (and certainly not to glorify) the existence of war but rather to acknowledge that these narratives are predicated on experiences of violence. John's audience is also thrust into a metaphorical battle.

Other Mothers: Jezebel and Babylon as Threatening Mothers

The first female figure a reader encounters in Revelation is "the woman Jezebel" (2:20), who is mentioned in the fourth of John's seven letters. The *ekklesia* in Thyatira is apparently familiar with her teachings. After praising the community's virtues ("love, faith, service, and endurance" [2:19]), the son of God says,

> But I have this against you, that you tolerate [or forgive; ἀφεῖς] the woman Jezebel, the one calling herself a prophet and teaching and misleading my slaves to fornicate and eat idol meat. I gave her time to repent, but she does not wish to repent of her fornication. Look, I am throwing her on a bed, and those who commit adultery with her I am throwing into great distress, unless they repent of her works, and I will kill her children, dead. (2:20–23)

John portrays this rival teacher as the foreign queen of Israel who encouraged King Ahab to convert to the worship of Baal and who killed Israelite prophets (1 and 2 Kings), thus emphasizing the differences between himself and Jezebel: She not only is misguided in her teaching but also teaches God's slaves to adulterate and to eat unclean food. This mother as educator is particularly dangerous because she instructs her children in the "wrong" practices, creating the wrong kind of community and a dangerous kind of tradition. John also sexualizes and genders her teaching and her punishment: She and her followers fornicate (πορνεῦσαι) and adulterate (μοιχεύοντας), and as punishment, she will be thrown on a bed.[173] Her children will not escape punishment, either; the speaker intends to kill them violently. The familial images are highlighted here because of the ways mother-child relationships imply continuity and similarity: Her children are, apparently, like her and her paramours, equally deserving of punishment. Thus, John insists on a particular kind of tradition and continuity as he condemns Jezebel for taking the community in a new, inappropriate direction by calling herself a prophet, promoting teachings that John sees as evil ("the deep things of Satan" [2:24]), and refusing to repent. Her pain is thus deserved "because she did not wish to turn from her fornication" (2:21).

---

[173] For a discussion of the meaning of "throw her on a bed," see Christopher A. Frilingos, *Spectacles of Empire: Monsters, Martyrs, and the Book of Revelation* (Philadelphia: University of Pennsylvania Press, 2004), 108–9.

Babylon, "the great whore" (17:1) is the third maternal figure in Revelation; like Jezebel, she is punished violently and sexually for her transgressions (17:16). She is "mother of whores and of earth's abominations [ἡ μήτηρ τῶν πορνῶν καὶ τῶν βδελυγμάτον τῆς γῆς]" (17:5). Her paramours are the kings of the earth who have "fornicated [ἐπόρνευσαν]" (17:2) with her; like Jezebel, her children share their mother's traits and wrongdoing; thus, they also share in the punishment inflicted on the maternal figure, as Babylon's power will turn on her eventually: The ten "horns," or kings who did not yet have kingdoms, would "make her desolate and naked, devour her flesh, and burn her up with fire" (17:16). The larger section focused on Babylon (chaps. 17–18) starkly contrasts the time when the inhabitants of Earth, including the kings, live luxuriously and fornicate with Babylon and the time when Earth will witness her destruction. In the latter, the ones who benefited from her luxurious life (the kings of the earth [18:9], the merchants of the earth [18:11], and the ones whose trade is connected to the sea [18:17]) mourn her torment; the "saints, apostles, and prophets" (18:20), however, are instructed to rejoice in her destruction. As with Jezebel and the Sun Woman, Babylon's motherhood transmits the essence of her identity to her children, guaranteeing continuity through reproduction: The children of Jezebel and Babylon are threatening because the mothers themselves are threatening, whereas the Sun Woman's son represents hope and promise, as she does. Moreover, when the mighty angel demonstrates Babylon's destruction by throwing a millstone into the sea, part of the prophecy includes the promise that "the voice of bridegroom and bride will be heard in you [Babylon] no more" (18:23), ensuring that there will be no more fecundity for the great city.

John's portrayal of Babylon as mother, city, whore, and woman relies on certain ancient tropes. Jennifer Glancy and Stephen Moore focus on the portrayal of Babylon as empress and, most especially, as prostitute. They argue, "John's representation of a whore seated as empress is designed to indict the empire itself, and this representation gains resonance from its location in the wider pattern of sexual invective characteristic of Roman political discourse. Understanding Babylon as βασίλισσα, we argue, requires that we give full weight to

John's designation of her as πόρνη."[174] In short, John's critique of Babylon/Rome is based on the empress being portrayed as a prostitute. Moreover, her portrayal is not as a single prostitute-empress but as a prostitute-empress with children. How does her portrayal as *porne* and as mother of *porne* affect how readers think of Babylon, especially as a mother? What kind of communal identity formation does this portrayal suggest? Studies of ancient prostitutes have shown the economic and social instability that precedes entry into prostitution; moreover, ancient rhetoric about prostitutes, especially prostitute mothers, is laced with suspicion and misogyny.[175] The title "mother of whores and of earth's abominations" not only indicates the "superlative" nature of her status as whore but also (and most especially) emphasizes that she is, in Shanell T. Smith's words, "the source—the creator of more just like her."[176] Her children, as children of a whore, a great empress, and an overthrown imperial system, are similarly cursed; like Jezebel's children, they will suffer the same fate as their mother. Whereas the Sun Woman's children guarantee the continuity of tradition, the violent death of Babylon and her children shows the abrupt end of the empire.

Although John invites the audience to think in binary terms, it is possible to acknowledge the ambivalence contained within this vision; the lives of Jezebel and Babylon, along with those of their (metaphorical) children, are in danger in this text. Moreover, the threat comes from heaven: The "son of God" (2:18) promises to destroy Jezebel, while "the ten horns," who are also "ten kings," will strip, eat, and burn her, because "God has put it into their hearts to carry out his purpose" (17:12, 16–17). Thinking about mothers in the FMLN and the desperate choices forced upon them in extreme circumstances complicates any attempt that we might make to dismiss

---

[174] Jennifer A. Glancy and Stephen D. Moore, "How Typical a Roman Prostitute Is Revelation's 'Great Whore'?" *Journal of Biblical Literature* 130, no. 3 (2011): 569.

[175] Strong, "Working Girls," 121–39.

[176] Shanell T. Smith, *The Woman Babylon and the Marks of Empire: Reading Revelation with a Postcolonial Womanist Hermeneutics of Ambiveilence* (Minneapolis, MN: Fortress, 2014), 140. David Aune understands "mother" in the superlative sense; see his *Revelation 17–22*, Word Biblical Commentary 52C (Nashville, TN: Thomas Nelson, 1998), 937.

Jezebel and Babylon as bad mothers who only corrupt their children. When considered alongside Salvadoran women combatants, Jezebel and Babylon emerge as both threatening and threatened mothers. They too are mothers in war, with all of the threat, violence, danger, and uncertainty that implies. Even though we tend to expect women to experience war through their sons or husbands, the FMLN women remind us that women are also sometimes combatants and survivors.

Ready to Conceive: The New Jerusalem as a Potential Mother

The New Jerusalem is the only feminine figure in Revelation who is not a mother; she is, instead, a bride (νύμφην; 21:2). Jerusalem is explicitly contrasted with Babylon; although "the voice of bride-groom and bride will be heard in [Babylon] no more" (18:23), here, the city herself is a bride—an untouched, inviolate city who is clean and pure. Virginity is an important metaphor for John, symbolizing preparedness, self-control, and cleanliness, so perhaps Jerusalem will remain chaste (or will conceive through parthenogenesis like Mary did?).[177] A bride indicates hope for the future and new beginnings, but in this text, she does so without consummation, reproduction, or offspring. She experiences no pain, punishment, or threat, unlike the other female figures in Revelation. Nothing but one tree of life grows in the New Jerusalem, which apparently has very little room for reproduction or change. There are no tears, pain, or death—thus, in some important ways, there seems to be no life. As John envisions

---

[177] "Compare with the ones who are 144,000 who have been redeemed from the earth in chap. 14; John writes, Then I looked, and there was the Lamb, standing on Mount Zion! And with him were one hundred and forty-four thousand who had his name and his Father's name written on their foreheads. And I heard a voice from heaven like the sound of many waters and like the sound of loud thunder; the voice I heard was like the sound of harpists playing on their harps, and they sing a new song before the throne and before the four living creatures and before the elders. No one could learn that song except the one hundred forty-four thousand who have been redeemed from the earth. It is these who have not defiled themselves with women, for they are virgins; these follow the Lamb wherever he goes. They have been redeemed from humankind as first fruits for God and the Lamb, and in their mouth no lie was found; they are blameless (Rev 14:1–5)."

it, the New Jerusalem has no room for mothers and their children, no productive pain, and no messy, broken bodies.

On the one hand, the bride might be read as a static figure, especially in the moments when this feminine figure is described explicitly as a city: New Jerusalem has "a great, high wall with twelve gates" (21:12), while the wall itself has "twelve foundations" (21:14). The stability and size of this city indicate the reassurance that is intended in John's vision: Jerusalem is stable and secure, so her inhabitants will be, too. It is also enormous, at 1,500 miles (12,000 stadia) long, wide, and tall. The bride Jerusalem herself speaks only once in 22:17, when, together with the Spirit, she says, "Come." This silent, imposing city, made of gold and jewels, is unmoving and unchanging. From this portrayal, an audience might anticipate that the bride will remain as she is: pure and inviolate.

On the other hand, given that *matrimonium* implies "an institution for making mothers (*matres*)," ancient audiences could have seen the New Jerusalem as a potential mother.[178] Indeed, a bride, especially one adorned with a veil, signifies the social transition "from virgin to matron" and the spatial transition to the new husband's house.[179] As the one coming down from heaven, "prepared as a bride adorned for her husband" (21:2), this bride is portrayed as ready to become a mother. Especially given that the other three female figures in Revelation are portrayed as mothers, perhaps the audience might also anticipate that this bride will bear Jerusalem's future offspring. As a bride, she is a liminal figure, on the threshold between pure virgin and potential mother.

Whether the emphasis lies on her virginity or her potential fecundity, the New Jerusalem still represents a contrast to the other female figures in Revelation; the other three, all maternal figures, face threats of violence to themselves and their children. The New Jerusalem, although she might be ready to conceive, is safe, at least for the moment. This difference suggests an important difference in

---

[178] Susan Treggiari, quoted in Genevieve Liveley, "*Mater Amoris*: Mothers and Lovers in Augustan Rome," in Petersen and Salzman-Mitchell, *Mothering and Motherhood in Ancient Greece and Rome*, 190.

[179] Lynn R. Huber, *Like a Bride Adorned: Reading Metaphor in John's Apocalypse* (New York: T & T Clark International, 2007), 128.

Revelation between maternal figures and nonmaternal female figures. Motherhood is presented as a threatened and threatening identity in John's Apocalypse, in that Revelation's mothers are consistently endangered and disregarded. As a non-mother, the New Jerusalem is not in danger in this text; only mothers and their children are vulnerable in John's vision.

Complex Maternal Identities

The maternal figures in Revelation emerge as endangered, complex figures. There is no straightforward "good mother" or "bad mother" in this text, only mothers who are being threatened with violence (sometimes with divine violence). None of them seems to survive the narrative violence: Jezebel and Babylon are threatened with violence from heaven, and the Sun Woman disappears. New Jerusalem, as bride, has not yet entered into a precarious maternal identity like the others that John describes. Revelation's mothers are used to reflect on the uses of suffering and loss, as well as the (dis)continuity of community relationships. Especially when we read this work alongside narratives from women in the FMLN, we see the ways in which Revelation's maternal figures are in complex, violent situations. Unlike the women in the FMLN, whose testimonials have been published and translated, the maternal figures in Revelation are narratively "disappeared" when their roles in the narrative are over.

Revelation's mythic mothers are part of a cosmic tale of heavenly violence, and these graphic (even pornographic) stories of mothers and their children might inure us to the real violence that women face in war.[180] The comparisons presented in this chapter between the female figures in Revelation and the women combatants in the FMLN cannot but be troubling: On the one hand, we have metaphorical female figures in an ancient text, and on the other hand, we have women who have endured unthinkable violence and loss while fighting in a war that ended only a generation ago and whose effects are still felt today. Even though the comparison is loose, the results of

---

[180] See Pippin's discussion of eroticized violence (as she calls it, "pornoapocalypse") in *Apocalyptic Bodies*, 92–97.

this juxtaposition have an important payoff for readers of Revelation: Recognizing the hardships of war helps us avoid glorifying wartime situations, even when they appear in religious texts. Moreover, readers do not sympathize easily with Jezebel or Babylon, but might considering the realities of war help us contextualize their stories differently and thus understand these narratives from a different angle?

The story of Rufina Amaya, the only known survivor of the infamous 1981 El Mozote massacre, underscores the tragedy of war and further punctuates my suggestion that we avoid glorifying wartime situations or glossing easily over (narrative) violence. Amaya's narrative shows the power of memory and testimony in communities trying to find hope after violence. Over the course of three days in December 1981, US-trained Salvadoran Army troops brutally killed more than one thousand civilians in the village of El Mozote. Although she was a noncombatant (unlike the mothers fighting in the FMLN), Amaya's testimonial has "assumed almost mythic dimensions" in the history of the Salvadoran Civil War.[181] Amaya said in her testimony during the Truth Commission for El Salvador,

> I could hear cries from the children, calling for their mothers. The soldiers were killing them too. They were hanging them, cutting their throats. I couldn't hear any shots, just the children's screams. Finally, I managed to get away. I didn't want to go, because I could still hear the children crying. . . . I was terribly upset, because I'd left my children behind: a boy aged nine, a girl aged five, one aged three and the baby who was just eight months. I still couldn't believe they'd kill them. . . . All the people were dead. . . . I was the only survivor of El Mozote. My four children and my husband were among those who were killed.[182]

---

[181] Leigh Binford, *The El Mozote Massacre: Anthropology and Human Rights* (Tucson: University of Arizona Press, 1996), 22.

[182] Mandy MacDonald and Mike Gatehouse, *In the Mountains of Morazon: Portrait of a Returned Refugee Community in El Salvador* (London: Latin American Bureau, 1995), 44.

After Amaya escaped, she "carved a little hole in the ground and stuck her face into it so that she could silently mourn her murdered family."[183] Her survival is, on the one hand, a hopeful moment to be celebrated—she did, after all, live through the ordeal—but on the other hand, her very presence evokes the memories of the hundreds of children, peasant farmers, and other noncombatants assassinated by government soldiers in El Mozote. As she says about her unlikely survival, "God allowed me to live so that I can testify how the Army killed the men and women and burned their children. I didn't see them kill the children, but I heard the children's screams."[184] Her presence points to inconceivable absence.

The maternal figures of Revelation, along with their children, provide testimonies that resonate with Amaya's story. The stories of violence that they and their children endure, followed by the figures' abrupt disappearances, are startling and unsettling, leaving readers to fill in the gaps of their unfinished stories. There is no happy ending for these figures, even if the end of Revelation is intended to provide hope and comfort to the audience. The maternal figures in John's Apocalypse can stand as reminders of the horrors of war and other abuses of power, even when the war originates from heaven and the punishment is from God. Rather than allowing them to quietly exit, we can allow Jezebel, the Sun Woman, and Babylon to provide testimony about the violence done to them and to their children. The disappearance of Revelation's maternal figures thus points us to other victims of war and to other disappeared children.

---

[183] Binford, *El Mozote Massacre*, 22.
[184] Wright, *El Salvador*, 21.

C H A P T E R   3

"Mother of the Nation": The Mother and Her Seven Sons in 4 Maccabees

In the ancient representations of the mother of the Maccabees, like traditions about Mary, themes of maternal suffering and sacrifice intersect with issues of choice, political domination, and resistance. Additionally, issues of ethnicity and race come to the fore in the Maccabean literature. In the various texts about the Maccabean mother and her children, maternal protection and devotion are presented as natural aspects of motherhood; these narratives about a mother who encourages her seven sons to die nobly are thus powerful advertisements for their cause, because she overrides what is apparently "natural" in order to remain faithful to their ancestral traditions. In this chapter, I demonstrate how the Maccabean mother's sacrifice of her sons and herself is particularly useful for these authors attempting to demonstrate the validity and nobility of their race, nation, and associated religious traditions.[185] I also discuss how linking maternal sacrifice to the cause of a nation creates a politically and emotionally charged space in which violence and suffering are memorialized. Not

---

[185] Maren Niehoff discusses nation, ethnicity, identity, and culture in her introduction to a work on Philo; like her, I assume that these ideas related to identity are social constructs. Moreover, scholarly discussions of these ideas are part of contemporary discourses about the modern nation-state. Niehoff writes, "All of these questions [about identity] are patently modern. They derive from relatively recent theories and are closely related to a burgeoning literature on ethnic identity and nationhood. . . . In Israel in particular such issues cannot be avoided by anyone consciously trying to understand his or her life in a wider intellectual context" (*Philo on Jewish Identity and Culture* [Tübingen: Mohr Siebeck, 2001], 1–5, quotation on 1). Although the nation-state is a modern phenomenon, I consciously use *nation* in this chapter to indicate both the ancient concepts of kingdom, peoplehood, or religious practices and the modern geopolitical concept.

only that, but through the process of remembering maternal suffering, the causes for that pain can be challenged or perpetuated, depending on who is memorializing the violence and for what reasons.

First, it is helpful to outline the story under consideration here. Although the narrative likely contains certain earlier oral and folkloric elements, the earliest extant text about the Maccabean mother is in 2 Maccabees, which famously contains the story of Hanukkah, dating probably from the mid-second to mid-first century BCE.[186] A later retelling in 4 Maccabees expands the comparatively briefer narratives from 2 Macc. 6–7 in the context of a philosophical discussion about the primacy of "devout reason" (ὁ εὐσεβὴς λογισμός). Scholars have traditionally dated 4 Maccabees to the mid-first century CE; however, more recent work on early Jewish and Christian texts has tended to date it to the early second century CE, thus making it contemporaneous with the Acts of the Apostles, Gospel of John, and letters of Ignatius.[187] Similar narratives about a mother and her seven sons who are killed by a tyrant are found in such later Jewish texts as *Lamentations Rabbah* 1:16 (circa fifth century CE), the Babylonian Talmud in Tractate *Gittin* 57b (circa seventh century CE), and *Sefer Josippon* (circa tenth century CE).[188] Even the medieval story of Rachel of Mainz seems to draw on similar narrative elements.

---

[186] See Robert Doran, "The Martyr: A Synoptic View of the Mother and Her Seven Sons," in *Ideal Figures in Ancient Judaism: Profiles and Paradigms*, ed. John J. Collins and George W. E. Nickelsburg (Missoula, MT: Scholars, 1980), 194; Robert Doran, "2 Maccabees," in *1 & 2 Maccabees, Job, Psalms*, vol. 4, New Interpreter's Bible (Nashville, TN: Abingdon, 1996), 240; Robert Doran, *2 Maccabees: A Critical Commentary*, Hermeneia (Minneapolis, MN: Augsburg Fortress, 2012), 14–15; and Daniel R. Schwartz, *2 Maccabees* (Berlin: Walter de Gruyter, 2008), 11–15.

[187] Elias Bickermann's argument (dating 4 Maccabees to 18–54 CE) was widely accepted for half a century, but Jan Willem van Henten has shown the problems with Bickermann's assumptions and has argued that the probable date is much later, perhaps around 100 CE. See his *The Maccabean Martyrs as Saviours of the Jewish People: A Study of 2 and 4 Maccabees* (Leiden: Brill, 1997), 73–78.

[188] See Gerard Rouwhorst, "The Cult of the Seven Maccabean Brothers and Their Mother in Christian Tradition," in *Saints and Role Models in Judaism and Christianity*, ed. Joshua Schwartz and Marcel Poorthuis (Boston: Brill, 2004), 183–204; Galit Hasan-Rokem, *Web of Life: Folklore and Midrash in Rabbinic Literature* (Stanford, CA: Stanford University Press, 2000); and Jan Willem van Henten, "The Christianization of the Maccabean Martyrs: The Case of Origen," in *Martyrdom and Persecution in Late Antique Christianity: Festschrift Boudewijn Dehandschutter*, ed. J. Leemans (Leuven: Uitgeverij Peeters, 2010), 333–51.

Christians also memorialize the Maccabean mother. Certain early Christian martyr acts, such as the *Letter of the Churches of Vienne and Lyon* (in the figure of Blandina) and the *Martyrdom of Montanus and Lucius*, reference the Maccabean mother-martyr as an exemplar. Origen, Cyprian, John Chrysostom, Ambrose, and Augustine all used the mother and her seven sons as examples of paradigmatic martyrs when their own flocks faced persecution or some other crisis. In his thirteenth-century *Golden Legend*, Jacobus de Voragine says it is notable that the Western Church venerates the "Holy Maccabees," because the Western Church typically "does not celebrate feasts of saints of the Old Testament, on the grounds that they descended into hell—exceptions being made for the Holy Innocents, in each of whom Christ was put to death, and for the Maccabees."[189] In these different versions of a similar narrative, shared notions of maternal self-sacrifice are used for considering ethnoreligious solidarity, philosophical ideas, and purported differences between Judaism and Christianity; that is, the narratives are "about" a mother and her sons who remain committed to their ancestral ways amid persecution, but the texts do other kinds of work, too.

The narratives follow a basic outline. First, a mother and her seven sons are brought before an oppressive ruler who demands that they renounce their ancestral customs and perform an act that would demonstrate loyalty to the ruler and the empire. (Earlier versions depict this action as eating pork, whereas some later narratives describe it as performing a sacrifice on behalf of the Roman emperor.) The ruler asks each son, in birth order, beginning with the eldest, to perform the action to preserve their life. As each son refuses, he is tortured and killed. The narratives consistently spend the most time on the seventh son and his speech, often emphasizing his young age (in some later versions, the mother even breastfeeds him before he is killed). Although he is young, he is able to give an eloquent rationale for why he will be faithful to his ancestral ways, his family, and his nation—before he, too, is tortured and killed. Finally, the mother herself dies, sometimes by suicide, sometimes at the torturers' hands. Although the (stated or implicit) goals of each narrative differ, the mother and her

---

[189] Jacobus de Voragine, *The Golden Legend: Readings on the Saints*, vol. 2, trans. William Granger Ryan, (Princeton, NJ: Princeton University Press, 1993), 33.

sons represent ideal figures in every case: They are pious or devout; Jewish (or, in later Christian sermons, ideally proto-Christian); and prime examples of self-control, courage, or (even in the mother's case) manliness. Foregrounding that these are idealized figures makes the goals and assumptions of the narratives much clearer.

Interpretive Issues: A Mother's Choices

In their considerations of the Maccabean mother, scholars have focused on a few key issues: the historicity of these narratives, whether or not these deaths should be considered martyrdoms, the ways in which these texts are involved in the so-called parting of the ways between Judaism and Christianity, the importance of nation and choice (including related or implied notions such as religion/philosophy, race/ethnicity, language, and ancestry), and the gendering of these characters, especially the mother. These issues shape scholarly interpretations of these texts, but highlighting our contemporary, post-Shoah context, including questions of Israeli and Palestinian identity, sheds new light on these issues and the ways in which our context shapes scholarly discussions.

A traditional view holds that this narrative, though certainly embellished, records some historically reliable details. Robin Darling Young's comments are typical of this view:

> There is no good reason to doubt that an actual mother of seven sons existed and was put to death publicly along with them; even the various tortures the family members endured are not implausible historical consequences. Yet it does seem likely that each author exercised some interpretation of the subject matter in order to present the particular significance of the martyrdoms for Jewish audiences . . . in each audience there were quite likely women for whom the mother, in her virtuous conduct and sacrifice, was meant to be a model to emulate.[190]

---

[190] Robin Darling Young, "The 'Woman with the Soul of Abraham': Traditions about the Mother of the Maccabean Martyrs," in *"Women Like This": New Perspectives on*

Daniel Schwartz argues differently: "As for historicity: while there definitely were martyrs in the Antiochian persecutions . . . no one would claim that this story as such is anything more than a stylized didactic narrative, perhaps deriving, ultimately, from a historicization of Jeremiah 15:9."[191] While they differ on whether a historical mother and seven sons persecuted in this particular manner lies behind this narrative, both scholars still emphasize the deaths of innocents in the Antiochian period.

The work of the Canadian scholar Suzanne Evans helps us reframe the historicity question. Evans encountered a similar issue in her investigation of the image of the "mother of martyrs," especially focusing on Canadian mothers of World War I soldiers. One particularly heartrending example that she encountered was a magazine article from Christmastime 1915. Entitled "I Am a Proud Mother This Christmas and I Will Tell You the Reason Why," the article was allegedly penned by a mother who had just received a telegram announcing the death of her son, a soldier. The mother wrote that she had been initially shocked and saddened by her son's death, but "that has gone. I am a proud mother this Christmas. For I gave Canada and the Empire a Christmas present. I gave them my chiefest possession. I yielded what was more than aught else in the world to me. I sacrificed the life of my boy."[192] Evans discovered in her research that no soldier by that name existed, and she concluded that even if the son were based on a real person, the story was simply war propaganda, capitalizing on maternal sacrifice. This display of national pride, comparable to that of the Spartan mothers discussed in chapter 1, summoned support for the war effort. Evans writes,

> Across cultures and historical eras, in times of great stress, societies will channel all resources, even maternal love, for

Jewish Women in the Greco-Roman World, ed. Amy-Jill Levine (Atlanta, GA: Scholars, 1991), 68.

[191] Schwartz, *2 Maccabees*, 299. Jeremiah 15:9 reads, "She who bore seven has languished; she has swooned away; her sun went down while it was yet day; she has been shamed and disgraced. And the rest of them I will give to the sword before their enemies, says the Lord."

[192] Suzanne Evans, *Mothers of Heroes, Mothers of Martyrs: World War I and the Politics of Grief* (Montreal: McGill-Queen's University Press, 2007), 86.

> a common cause. . . . Whatever the mix of public pressure,
> opinion, and religious values, and whatever the directives
> of their own hearts, many people were faced with agoniz-
> ing choices. Yet the focus of this study is the mothers of
> the fallen and how their stories have been used and modi-
> fied in different historical contexts to create a martyrology.
> These stories, used by master propagandists to unite society
> in the waging of war, still maintain their grip. They retain
> their power to shock, appall and compel—which is pre-
> cisely what all martyrologists are aiming for.[193]

Her work shows how notions of maternal love and sacrifice were channeled to increase support for World War I and the ruling powers in Canada and Europe, rather than simply being an expression of maternal nature. The story of the mother of the Maccabees can easily be read the same way; in fact, reading it as a kind of propaganda changes the historicity question. Rather than asking, "Does this narrative refer to historical events?" it is more fruitful to ask, "What purpose did this narrative serve in its historical context, and what are the other, unintended consequences of the way the story is told?" In this framing, the question of whether this story really happened becomes unimportant; the story is recounted in a particular historical moment and does rhetorical work for the author(s), just as the Canadian magazine article used maternal love and sacrifice to increase support for the war effort. Martyrologists thus use the bonds between family and nationalism as rhetorical devices.[194]

A related and contentious question is whether the figures in 4 Maccabees can be called martyrs; moreover, this definitional issue is not an abstract question with no consequences in our contemporary situation. The question of whether to call these figures martyrs is related to modern Jewish and Christian identities, especially post-Shoah, a

---

[193] Ibid., x.

[194] Elizabeth Castelli's work on martyrdom likewise problematizes questions of historicity in martyrdom narratives and shows the rhetorical work that martyrologists do (see her *Martyrdom and Memory: Early Christian Culture Making* [New York: Columbia University Press, 2004]).

topic I consider more below. Modern scholars often describe these figures as martyrs, even though neither 2 nor 4 Maccabees uses μάρτυς or its cognates in their technical senses.[195] The issue may seem to be straightforward: Christians (more precisely, Catholic and Orthodox Christians) venerate these figures as martyrs, whereas Jews do not. This acknowledges certain historical realities, especially related to the canonization and transmission of texts. Martyrdom is just one example of the contested and constructed borders between Christians and Jews in antiquity, however; as Daniel Boyarin has effectively demonstrated, "martyrdom as a discourse was shared and fought over between rabbinic Judaism and Christianity as these two complexly intertwined religions and social formations were approaching their definitive schism in Eusebius's fourth century."[196] Seeing martyrdom as a shared and contested discourse in antiquity, and today, albeit differently, helps us to understand that the question of whether to call these figures martyrs does not always split easily along Jewish/Christian lines.[197]

Affirming that these figures did indeed die as martyrs is a way to assign meaning to innocent deaths in oppressive contexts; it grants them value and importance rather than rendering their deaths meaningless or simply tragic. For example, scholars such as Tessa Rajak give meaning to these deaths specifically as *Jewish* deaths and highlight the martyrs' importance as national heroes. She asserts that 4 Maccabees "undoubtedly" constitutes a martyrology, "even in the absence in the text of the term itself or of any Greek equivalent."[198] In 4 Maccabees, she sees "the essential

---

[195] See, for example, Doran, "The Martyr"; Young, "Woman with the Soul of Abraham"; van Henten, *Maccabean Martyrs*; and Susan Haber, "Living and Dying for the Law: The Mother-Martyrs of 2 Maccabees," *Women in Judaism: A Multidisciplinary Journal* 4, no. 1 (Winter 2006), all of which declare these figures "martyrs" even in the titles. This is often done in collusion with ancient Christian sources that refer to the "holy Maccabean martyrs."

[196] Daniel Boyarin, *Dying for God: Martyrdom and the Making of Christianity and Judaism* (Stanford, CA: Stanford University Press, 1999), 114.

[197] See Daniel Joslyn-Siemiatkoski's introduction, "Remembering the Maccabean Martyrs," in *Christian Memories of the Maccabean Martyrs* (New York: Palgrave Macmillan, 2009), 1–12.

[198] Tessa Rajak, "Dying for the Law: The Martyr's Portrait in Jewish-Greek Literature," in *Portraits: Biographical Representation in the Greek and Latin Literature of the Roman Period*, ed. M. J. Edwards and Simon Swain (Oxford: Clarendon Press, 1997), 40.

attributes of the Jewish martyr."[199] Rajak takes issue with scholars who see Jewish martyrdom literature paving the way for Christian narratives of martyrdom, arguing instead that martyrdom narratives serve dramatically different purposes for Jews and Christians.[200] She describes Christian martyrs as "powerful advertisement[s]" used for "propagating the faith," while describing Jewish martyrs as "national heroes or heroines" who "served to encapsulate state-ments about national identity, to define the nation's relation to outsiders and to explore potential political crises."[201] As part of her argument that the Maccabees died distinctively as Jewish mar-tyrs, she urges, "The children of Abraham and their prize-winning mother [compare with 4 Macc. 18:23] ought to be restored to the bosom of Abraham and to the choirs of their fathers where they belong."[202]

Unlike Rajak, Boyarin emphasizes the fuzzy, contested bor-ders between Christian and Jewish martyrs and, likewise, between Christianity and Judaism, which he sees as closely related siblings:

> The martyrdom of the mother and her seven sons in 4 Maccabees, I would propose, was produced in the same religious atmosphere, the same (Asian?) religious environ-ment, in which figures such as Ignatius and Polycarp (and perhaps even the Martyrs of Lyons) lived and breathed. And if, as Bowersock confidently presumes, "the two stories in the books of the Maccabees have nothing to do either with the authentic history of the Maccabees or with the lost original text that recounted it," but "have everything to do with the aspirations and literature of the early Christians," they have everything do with the aspirations and literature of contemporary Jews, as well. How could they not?[203]

---

[199] Ibid.
[200] See, for example, W. H. C. Frend, *Martyrdom and Persecution in the Early Church: A Study of a Conflict from the Maccabees to Donatus* (Oxford: Blackwell, 1965).
[201] Rajak, "Dying for the Law," 67.
[202] Ibid.
[203] Boyarin, *Dying for God*, 115.

Boyarin's insights enable scholars to see the ways in which these texts (among others) function as part of the rhetorical and discursive boundary-making process between what would later be called Judaism and Christianity; this contrasts strongly with an approach like that of Rajak, who sees clear, decisive boundaries between Christians and Jews and knows exactly on which side the Maccabean martyrs belong.[204]

We must carefully acknowledge, then, that it is in the telling and retelling that these narratives become martyrdoms. If the characters are historical figures at all, they would not have been thought of as martyrs by their contemporaries but only in later moments of commemoration; as Elizabeth Castelli says, "Martyrdom requires audience (whether real or fictive), retelling, interpretation, and world- and meaning-making activity."[205] Even today, these texts are again made into martyrdoms, as the figures are remembered in various contexts, including as boundary makers between Judaism and Christianity.

Scholars commonly distinguish between the Jewish origins of the narrative and the later Christian cult associated with the Maccabean mother and sons, though this firm distinction neither is helpful for adequately explaining the history of this narrative nor takes into account the diverse nature of ancient Judaism (which includes the earliest Christians) and the complex ideological process that often goes by the name "parting of the ways." While 2 Maccabees is almost certainly a "Jewish" document in origin (that is, it predates Jesus and, thus, Christians), 4 Maccabees is likely from a time when certain Jews and others were being called Christian.[206] Moreover, these texts were later preserved by Christian scribes in Christian canons, thus complicating the notion that even 2 Maccabees is simply a Jewish text. We have not yet developed an adequate vocabulary to describe the complex and

---

[204] Ibid., esp. 93–126; see also Boyarin's *Border Lines: The Partition of Judaeo-Christianity* (Philadelphia: University of Pennsylvania Press, 2004).

[205] Castelli, *Martyrdom and Memory*, 34.

[206] For an extensive discussion of the nuances of Ἰουδαῖος (Greek) and *Iudaeus* (Latin) in antiquity, see Shaye J. D. Cohen, *The Beginnings of Jewishness: Boundaries, Varieties, Uncertainties* (Berkeley: University of California Press, 1999), 69–106; see also Steve Mason, "Jews, Judaeans, Judaizing, Judaism: Problems of Categorization in Ancient History," *Journal for the Study of Judaism* 38, no. 4 (2007): 457–512. For an argument that Judaism as a religion was interpellated by Christians in antiquity see Boyarin, *Border Lines*, 9–13.

divergent entities of the first few centuries CE. These texts idealize fig-ures who prioritize their religious commitments (connected to nation and race), but these texts themselves also represent a place of discursive boundary making between Christians and Jews.

Four Maccabees represents a site of border disputes between Christians and Jews, in both the devotional cult of the Maccabees and the transmission of the stories themselves. The books of the Maccabees have been transmitted through the centuries by Christian scribes (though they are not listed in most extant canon lists[207]), even while the Jewish sages tell the story of Miriam bat Tanhum and her seven sons in *Lamentations Rabbah* and in the Babylonian Talmud. These later Jewish narratives have been interpreted in ways that indicate reli-gious "competition" and interreligious invective. For example, in the narrative from the fifth-century text *Lamentations Rabbah*, Miriam bat Tanhum tells her seventh son, "My son, go tell Abraham, our father, 'My mother says to you, "Do not take pride, claiming, I built an altar and offered up my son Isaac. Now see, my mother built seven altars and offered up seven sons in one day. And yours was only a test, but I really had to do it"' (*Lam. Rabbah* 1:16)."[208] Even though it is addressed to Abraham, the mother's speech is also implicitly directed at the Virgin Mary, and thus Christians: folklorist Galit Hasan-Rokem argues, "The comparison clearly implies that [Miriam bat Tanhum's] suffering is even greater than that of Mary, the mother of Jesus (the names are, of course, identical), who sacrificed 'only' one son, unlike her seven."[209] Christian belief in the doctrine of the resurrection may also make it seem as though Mary did not "really have to do it," because her son does not remain dead, as the seven sons do.[210]

---

[207] Daniel Joslyn-Siemiatoski, "2 Maccabees and 4 Maccabees: Textual Receptions in the Early Medieval West" (paper presented at the annual meeting for the Society of Biblical Literature, San Francisco, November 19–22, 2011).

[208] Translation from Jacob Neusner, *Lamentations Rabbah: An Analytical Translation* (Atlanta, GA: Scholars, 1989).

[209] Hasan-Rokem, *Web of Life*, 125; see also Joslyn-Siemiatkoski (*Christian Memories of the Maccabean Martyrs*, 125–26), who discusses the ways in which the Aqedah was often associated with Jesus's crucifixion in early Christianity.

[210] Although 2 Maccabees includes references to the idea of resurrection (for example, 2 Maccabees 7:23, when the mother says to her sons, "Therefore the Creator of the

The Maccabean martyrs have been venerated in various Christian traditions: fourth-century Antioch served as one cult center, and medieval Cologne served as another, and relics of these martyrs are purported to be in a variety of places.[211] They were typically memorialized as a family unit, sometimes with Eleazar as the patriarch. Many scholars have noted that this veneration is "remarkable"; Gerard Rouwhorst's assessment is typical: "It is rather surprising that Christians venerated Jews who were not simply pious or morally outstanding persons, but who suffered martyrdom for the sake of a commandment which according to most Christians had lost its relevance after Christ, namely the eating of pig meat."[212] Rouwhorst's assumption that Jews and Christians are fully separate, bounded entities glosses over the many groups in antiquity that blurred those boundaries. For example, he takes for granted that only Jews kept kosher, even given the existence of groups in antiquity that, in Ignatius's words, "proclaim Christ and Judaize" (*To the Magnesians*, 10.3). According to Ignatius, doing so is "monstrous" or "outlandish" (literally, "out of place," [ἀτοπόν]), but references to ancient groups that blurred the boundary between Jews and Christians complicate the assumptions that Rouwhorst and others make about the Christian cult devoted to the Maccabees. Christian veneration of the Maccabean mother and brothers need not be so surprising if one assumes that the words of the powerful bishops who strove to make a strong difference between Christianity and Judaism were not indicative of everyday Christians' practices and beliefs. The bishops' words were meant to be normative, of course, but indicate that people were doing the opposite of what the bishops wanted. Indeed, the sermons from John Chrysostom indicate that Antioch itself was a site of very unclear boundaries between "Judaism" and "Christianity," so the fact that Christians venerated these saints, in Antioch and elsewhere, is not at all remarkable.[213]

---

world, who shaped the beginning of humankind and devised the origin of all things, will in his mercy give life and breath back to you again"), 4 Maccabees does not.
[211] See Joslyn-Siemiatkoski, *Christian Memories of the Maccabean Martyrs*, 42–50, 137–51.
[212] Rouwhorst, "Cult of the Seven Maccabean Brothers," 184.
[213] See Joslyn-Siemiatkoski, *Christian Memories of the Maccabean Martyrs*, 42–50; Leonard V. Rutgers, "The Importance of Scripture in the Conflict Between Jews and

Texts about the mother and her seven sons, then, are not indicative of already-parted ways but instead are one place where those constructed borders are imposed.

Partially at issue in discussions of Judaism and Christianity in antiquity is the notion of choice as it relates to religion, nation, and ethnicity. Scholars often consider whether the Maccabean mother and her seven sons had a choice in their response to the king's demand. To be sure, the king seems to offer them a choice—"You will have positions of authority in my government *if you will renounce* the ancestral tradition of your national life. Enjoy your youth by *adopting* the Greek way of life and by *changing* your manner of living" (4 Macc. 8:7b–8; emphasis added)—but scholars analyzing this offer often emphasize (1) that religion, race/ethnicity, and political commitments overlap for the mother and sons only *because* they are Jewish (which contrasts with interpretations of Perpetua and Felicitas, who are thought to choose their Christian identity) and (2) that because of this, death at the king's hand was inevitable, so their only choice was *how* they would die. Interpretations of Christian martyrs hinge on notions of choice, even though interpreters assume that Jews in antiquity would have been somehow more conspicuous and their identity more immutable than those of Christians. Judith Lieu, for example, suggests that "Judaism demanded a loyalty of belief and life that could lead to death itself and set the Jewish people apart from all other peoples."[214] Shaye Cohen, however, has convincingly argued that Judeans/Jews were largely indistinguishable from other groups in antiquity.[215]

In addition to this, Denise Kimber Buell's work on ethnic reasoning presents Christians, Jews, and "pagans" as *all* using various

---

Christians: The Example of Antioch," in *The Use of Sacred Books in the Ancient World*, ed. Leonard V. Rutgers, Pieter W. van der Horst, and Lieve M. Teugels (Bondgenotenlaan, Leuven: Peeters, 1998), 287–303.

[214] Judith Lieu, *Image and Reality: The Jews in the World of the Christians in the Second Century* (Edinburgh: T & T Clark, 1996), 85.

[215] In his words, "How did you know a Jew in antiquity when you saw one? You did not." He goes on to argue that one could make guesses, based on ritual, socializing with other Jews, and so on, but emphasizes that even seemingly clear markers (for example, circumcision or dietary practices) were not guaranteed signals in one way or another (see Cohen, *Beginnings of Jewishness*, 67).

forms of ethnoracial logic and language to discuss topics that moderns would classify as religious.[216] Buell shows that ancient sources treat ethnicity/race as "both fixed and fluid."[217] Rather than describing Judaism as an ethnicity (that includes religious practices) and Christianity as only a religion (that transcends race/ethnicity), Jews and Christians in antiquity capitalized on fixity and fluidity when they described membership and participation in their groups. The author of 4 Maccabees participated in this larger trend of ethnic reasoning by presenting the mother and brothers as able to choose renunciation (fluidity) but remaining committed to their ancestral traditions, in part because they are descended from common ancestors, like Abraham (fixity).

In the past decade, several scholars in religious studies have argued that "religion" as a disembedded category of human experience is a recent, and particularly Christian, invention.[218] In antiquity (and likewise, in many times and places since), religion was inseparable from culture, tradition, politics, and racial/ethnic identity. It is anachronistic, then, for scholars of antiquity to refer to ancient Judaism and Christianity simply as religions, as if that category would have been as intelligible for ancients as it is for moderns. Rather, we should acknowledge that references to εὐσέβεια, *religio*, *pietas*, and so on would have encompassed far more than what moderns typically mean by "religion" (that is, a chosen, individualized commitment to a particular belief system).[219] Notions of choice related to both nation and religion are even more complicated when considering the history of statehood in Palestine and Israel, considered below.

Maternal Activists Engaging the Nation

Contemporary maternal activists often wrestle with issues that the narratives of the Maccabean mother evoke, including choice,

---

[216] Denise Kimber Buell, *Why This New Race? Ethnic Reasoning in Early Christianity* (New York: Columbia University Press, 2005).

[217] Ibid., 36.

[218] Ibid., 59; and Boyarin, *Border Lines*, 8–13. Boyarin, inter alia, shows that the roots of the invention of "religion" belong to Late Antiquity.

[219] Buell, *Why This New Race?* 60.

nationhood, gender, and identity. Moreover, contemporary commentators and analysts (whether in media, academia, pop culture,
or elsewhere) often critique maternal activists for their willingness
to put abstract causes ahead of their children's well-being. Cindy
Sheehan, for example, became a high-profile antiwar activist after
her son Casey was killed in action in April 2004 and she famously
camped outside of then-president George W. Bush's Texas ranch for a
month, demanding a meeting with him and protesting the Iraq War.
Sheehan endured public shame for activism, mostly because she had
three surviving children at home.[220]

Although Sheehan is a good analog, the Maccabean mother's
actions are even more extreme: Instead of simply "neglecting" her
children in order to resist an oppressive tyrant, she encourages her
children to die in their own acts of resistance. Both Gail Streete and
Carolyn Osiek make the striking comparison between the Maccabean
mother and the mothers of suicide bombers.[221] Streete discusses
the ways in which women's words (of both female suicide attackers and mothers of suicide attackers) are later used for propagan-
distic purposes. Likewise, Osiek, in her consideration of the mother
in 2 Maccabees 7, writes, "The same behavior can be seen in some
Palestinian mothers, like that of a 'martyr' featured recently in the
Western press, who says in the presence of her remaining sons: 'I
hope they will all do the same.'"[222] This comparison between the
Maccabean mother and mothers of suicide bombers is unsettling but,
in many ways, apt: The mother's encouragement results in her children's deaths, and *she rejoices in that.*

Like mothers of martyrs, female suicide attackers are also often
seen as paradoxical figures; in journalist Barbara Victor's words,
a female suicide attacker moves from "bearer of life to killing
machine."[223] One of the most famous suicide attackers, Wafa Idris,

---

[220] Wilson, "From Gestation to Delivery," 231–52.
[221] See Gail P. C. Streete, "Why Martyrs Matter," in *Redeemed Bodies: Women Martyrs in Early Christianity* (Louisville, KY: Westminster John Knox, 2009), 103–22, and Carolyn Osiek, "*Pietas* in and out of the Frying Pan," *Biblical Interpretation* 11, no. 2 (2003): 169.
[222] Osiek, "*Pietas* in and out of the Frying Pan," 169.
[223] Barbara Victor, *Army of Roses: Inside the World of Palestinian Women Suicide Bombers* (Emmaus, PA: Rodale, 2003), 33.

the first *shahida* in the Second Intifada, was a twenty-six-year-old Red Crescent volunteer and a divorced mother of a child who had died.[224] Much of the rhetoric, especially in Western media, has focused on Idris's personal life—for example: "some people argue that given her status as a divorcee, Idris was forced into martyrdom by her conservative society."[225] Many other female suicide attackers, however, have been married, and most have living children, even grandchildren. Their actions, then, cannot simply be attributed to social shame or ostracism within their communities. Like the suicide bombers and their mothers, the Maccabean mother is situated in a deeply oppressive context. These figures point to the complexity of representations of women and children in violent contexts.

By foregrounding the violent context in which the Maccabean mother is placed, we can resist the easy assessments often made about her (and other mothers in similarly intolerable situations); she is neither simply heroic nor simply villainous. She is like many mothers, before and since, who have acted in a way that seems incomprehensible to outsiders not living in an impossibly difficult circumstance. The narrator of 4 Maccabees even dictates the "cowardly" speech she *could* have given but did not (see 16:5–11 and below). Rather than celebrating the mother as straightforwardly brave and admirable, we can choose to read her as akin to a maternal activist who wants what is best for her children but does not live in a world that guarantees their lives or safety. In the midst of that sort of situation, she encourages her sons to die in a way that grants their lives (and deaths) meaning. For contemporary interpreters, this text is haunted by the specter of terrorism; rhetoric and actions on behalf of a nation (whether that nation is a recognized state or not) can have dire consequences.

Focusing on this maternal figure as if she really does have agency and reasoning momentarily occludes the constructed nature of this text and the ways in which the author shaped these figures. If this

---

[224] Yasser Arafat coined the Arabic word *shahida* (feminine form of *shahid*, "martyr") on January 27, 2002, in a speech to Palestinian women in Ramallah. Idris carried out her suicide attack the same day (see ibid., 19–20).

[225] Shannon Dunn, "The Female Martyr and the Politics of Death: An Examination of the Martyr Discourses of Vibia Perpetua and Wafa Idris," *Journal of the American Academy of Religion* 78, no. 1 (March 2010): 212n26.

mother came to us unmediated and we could actually see her actions "as they were," that would be a different matter, but we cannot do so. She is part and parcel of a philosophical argument, and we must evaluate her on those terms. In that literary context, what does it mean that the narrator praises the Maccabean mother's maternal love while also celebrating her sacrifice? What are the consequences for audiences (both ancient and modern) when a mother is memorialized for encouraging her children to die for a cause for which she also perished? What maternal comportments are reinscribed as honorable or valorous if the Maccabean mother is presented as ideal? What happens to a nation/religion/people that valorizes a mother who loses her sons?

Four Maccabees does not mourn or remember the Maccabean mother or her sons in an exclusively grief-filled tone. Rather, the author celebrates her for being an honorable, masculine mother and remembers her sons for their bravery. We see this difference in two approaches to Memorial Day and other similar holidays: Is it a celebration of the armed forces or a solemn memorial in honor of the war dead? At substantial distance from the loss, such commemorations often become celebrations, rose-colored remembrances of bravery, heroism, and struggle—indeed, vehicles for nationalism that promote an unquestioning stance toward the nation. This is accomplished without a real acknowledgment of the substantial losses that war entails. The rhetoric of these ancient texts similarly focuses on the admirable bravery of the mother and her sons without highlighting the loss, struggle, mourning, and protest.

The Maccabean Mother, Maternal Self-Sacrifice, and the Nation

As an expansion and reworking of 2 Maccabees, the story in 4 Maccabees follows a similar narrative arc, beginning with Eleazar (5:1–7:23), next focusing on the seven brothers (8:1–14:10), and ending with the mother (14:11–18:24). The beginning four chapters are philosophical arguments for the thesis stated in 1:1, "that pious reason is absolute master of the passions [εἰ αὐτοδέσποτός ἐστιν τῶν παθῶν ὁ εὐσεβὴς λογισμός]." These nine figures who die rather than "renounce Judaism [ἐξόμνυσθαι τὸν Ιουδαϊσμόν]" (4:26) by "tasting

the meat of swine and of things sacrificed to idols" (5:2) are the narrative proof of that thesis because they are able to master their passions
(including fraternal and maternal love) with divine reason.[226] After
Eleazar is killed, the boys are brought forward (as in 2 Maccabees and
elsewhere, in birth order), "handsome, modest, noble, and graced in
every way," along with their "aged mother" (8:3).

The figure of the mother exemplifies the deep connections
among familial devotion, religious commitment, and national pride.
The Maccabean mother, as an example of εὐσέβεια, demonstrates her
piety in and through her devotion to her family (and her chastity).
Like its Latin counterpart *pietas*, εὐσέβεια combines notions of family values, loyalty to a kinship group or nation, and religious obser-
vance.[227] This deep imbrication of family, nation, and religion is
most obvious in the Augustan marriage legislation, which is one of
the clearest examples of the ancient idealization and politicization
of motherhood. These laws promoted marriage and childbearing
(especially for elites) as good for the empire, giving material rewards
for both.[228] Likewise, the iconography of the Ara Pacis Augustae and
other similar images elevate idealized motherhood and harmonious
family life as both pious and patriotic. The official encouragement of
motherhood, along with its idealization, were presented as good for
the family and the empire alike; moreover, family commitments and
religious devotion were mutually co-constituting.

The ways in which the Maccabean mother encourages her sons in
their commitment to the ancestral laws, her references to Torah, and her
admonishment that her sons "have faith in God and not be grieved"
(16:22) all exemplify the ideal of εὐσέβεια, especially for a *materfamilias*. Moreover, the brief mention of her husband in a speech to her
sons "guarantees her chastity;" thus she is also an idealized *univira*
("one-man woman"), or wife of only one husband.[229] Although modern readers sometimes express surprise that she expresses her familial
devotion by encouraging her sons to accept death, the ancient ideal

---

[226] This is the only attestation of Ἰουδαϊσμός in 4 Maccabees. In 2 Maccabees, it is used
three times (2:21; 8:1; 14:38). (See Mason, "Jews, Judaeans, Judaizing, Judaism," 464.)
[227] D'Angelo, "*Eusebeia*," 141.
[228] Dixon, *Roman Mother*, 72.
[229] D'Angelo, "*Eusebeia*," 156.

of a formidable mother included what moderns might call "maternal severity" and did not preclude acceptance of a child's death.[230]

The εὐσέβεια of the Maccabean mother is one example of the ways in which 4 Maccabees is a text that includes both accommodation and resistance[231]; this is also true, though with important differences, for 2 Maccabees. Both texts advocate a resistant posture toward imperial rule and foreign domination. Moreover, they demand wholehearted commitment to the ancestral customs, especially in resisting sacrifice to other deities and consumption of pork, yet in their resistance, the texts reinscribe and valorize many of the ideals espoused by the empire they seem to be resisting. These figures' deaths function similarly to Hellenistic and Roman practices of *devotio*, ensuring further success for their nation.[232] "Indeed," Mary Rose D'Angelo notes, "defiance itself must in a sense speak the language of the oppressor," and the mother of 4 Maccabees literally does that: In Greek, she instructs her sons in values recognizable to and valued by the soldiers (such that "Antiochus proclaimed the endurance of those people to his own soldiers as an example" [4 Macc 17:23–24]).[233]

The mother is mentioned only briefly in the chapters that focus on her sons: As he is about to be tortured, the third brother says, "Do you not know that the same father begat me along with those who are now dead, and the same mother gave birth to me and trained me on the same principles?" (10:2; cf. sixth brother in 11:15). The mother connects her sons both biologically and pedagogically, a point that is emphasized again in 13:20–21 in a discussion of the maternal womb (discussed below). The author of 4 Maccabees rearranges certain parts of the narrative from 2 Maccabees to put all the material about the mother together; when the king summons the mother "in order that, taking pity on herself, bereft of so many sons, she might urge the remaining one [the seventh son] on to life-saving obedience" (12:6), the narrator reports that the mother exhorted him in Hebrew but says, "as we will recount a little later" (12:7).

---

[230] Ibid., 148; see also Dixon, *Roman Mother*, preface, 233–36.
[231] D'Angelo, "Eusebeia," 163–64.
[232] Shmuel Shepkaru, *Jewish Martyrs in the Pagan and Christian Worlds* (New York: Cambridge University Press, 2006), 47–48.
[233] D'Angelo, "Eusebeia," 164.

The transitional section between the seven brothers and their mother is encomiastic and is also more straightforwardly philosophical than narrative in genre. Here, the maternal body is invoked most obviously: when the author attempts to demonstrate the strength of fraternal love, he is unable to do so without reference to their mother. Fraternal bonds are "implanted in the maternal womb" (14:19), the place where the brothers "having dwelt for the same amount of time, having been molded at the same time, having been strengthened from the same blood, and having been brought to ripeness through the same soul, and having been brought to full term through the same amount of time, and nursing on milk from the same springs, from which embraces the brother-loving souls were compacted together" (13:20–21). This embodied discourse configures the maternal body, specifically the womb and breasts, as a common experience that leads the brothers to feel affectionately toward one another, thus the maternal body and its "natural" properties are necessary parts of the author's philosophical argument; the mother's body exemplifies her devotion to her sons while also guaranteeing their similar character as an example of communal continuity. When Hasan-Rokem discusses the rhetorical import of the maternal body in other martyrological narratives, she argues,

> The intimacy of the mother-infant relationship creates the starkest possible contrast with the torture and execution arena. The oppressive violence of the representative of earthly authority is the radical opposite of the physical devotion conveyed by the motherly body. . . . No tale about a male martyr could throw into such high relief the presence of birth as the absolute antithesis of death, albeit death as an ideal, as does the tale of a martyred woman, especially a nursing mother.[234]

Here, the maternal body also serves as a synecdoche for both the development and continuity of a community (the similarity of the

---

[234] Hasan-Rokem, *Web of Life*, 123. Her analysis of the rhetorical impact of breastfeeding and maternal embodiment applies equally well to the narratives about Perpetua and Felicitas (see chap. 4).

sons is ensured through her blood and her milk) and the creation of
relationships within a group.

The narrator praises the mother for being both like and unlike
a mother, saying, "Mothers become more sympathetic than fathers
from their sufferings for those born from them" (15:4). This mother,
because she suffered through seven pregnancies and labors, "loved
her children more than all mothers" (15:6), yet her "fear of God [τὸν
θεόν φόβον]" (15:8) wins out, ultimately, over her maternal affections,
even though her sons' "nobility and goodness" actually increases her
love for her sons! This test, according to the author, was more difficult
than birthing the sons in the first place (15:16) and was also "more
severe than that of each of her sons."[235] By connecting suffering and
love, the author demonstrates the strength of both: The mother's love
is great because her suffering is great, and vice versa—and yet, her
pious reasoning is even greater than her love or her suffering.

In 15:20, a notable textual discrepancy reveals that certain versions of 4 Maccabees emphasize this connection between birth and
death in the mother's anguish. Although Alfred Rahlfs's critical edi-
tion (upon which the RSV, NRSV, and so on are based) simply says
that the mother "saw the place" (τὸ χωρίον) of the boys' torture, the
Sinaiticus manuscript reads that she saw the "after birth" (χόριον).[236]
David DeSilva writes,

> Given this author's lack of reserve when it comes to sparing
> his audience's sensibilities [in narrating the violent torture
> of each figure], I would be inclined to read the Sinaiticus
> text as inviting the hearers to perceive the space, with the
> mother, as a place where her children have been trans-
> formed into their own afterbirths (i.e., biological waste
> matter) and the place transformed into their mass grave
> (even though it would not be their *final* resting place).[237]

[235] David A. DeSilva, *4 Maccabees: Introduction and Commentary on the Greek Text in
Codex Sinaiticus*, Septuagint Commentary Series (Leiden: Brill, 2006), 218.
[236] Ibid., 224–25. See also Alfred Rahlfs, *Septuaginta* (Stuttgart: Deutsche
Bibelgesellschaft, 1935).
[237] DeSilva, *4 Maccabees*, 225.

This deliberate linking of natural birth with death and with eternal life demonstrates the necessity of using a maternal figure in this narrative. A father or other close relative would not suffice for the rhetorical purposes of certain key elements of this text; the author requires a mother, in whom pain and fecundity are linked, for his argument. The pain of childbirth, or death under oppression, is not final, for either this mother or her nation. As one who suffered in childbirth and then suffers exceedingly at her children's deaths, a maternal figure is crucial for showing the power of pious reason, such that she is able to "disregard her temporal love for her children" (15:23, DeSilva's translation).

The emphasis on the masculinity of the mother is surprising, then, in light of the ways in which the author highlights the maternal body. In 4 Maccabees, the maternal body is both a paradigmatically weak place and, in this mother's case, a place of incredible strength; thus, her maternal body is paradoxically masculine. Scholars of ancient Greco-Roman gender have highlighted the connections among masculinity and endurance, bravery, virtue, self-mastery, and control. These connections are perhaps most obvious in such Greek and Latin words as ἀνδρεία ("courage"; with the same root as ἀνήρ, "man") and *virtus* ("virtue," "bravery," "strength"; with the same root as *vir*, "man"). Thus, when the mother is portrayed as exceedingly brave, "more manly than males" (4 Macc. 15:30), she appears even more masculine than the tyrant, Antiochus IV Epiphanes, even though she is female. In effect, this portrayal both feminizes Antiochus and masculinizes the mother (and her seven sons and the elderly man, Eleazar). For example, after Eleazar, the seven brothers, and the mother die, Antiochus, "when he saw the courage of their virtue and their endurance under the tortures [τὴν ἀνδρείαν αὐτῶν τῆς ἀρετῆς καὶ τὴν ἐπὶ ταῖς βασάνοις ὑπομονὴν], proclaimed them to his soldiers as an example for their own endurance" (17:23). By imperial standards, then, she is even more masculine than a(n ideal) man. In addition, by extension, "observant Jews are a superior race of 'men' (even when they happen to be anatomically female), since they are ruled not by reason alone but by 'devout reason' (ὁ εὐσεβὴς λογισμός), reason subservient to the Torah."[238] This

---

[238] Stephen D. Moore and Janice Capel Anderson, "Taking It like a Man: Masculinity in 4 Maccabees," *Journal of Biblical Literature* 117, no. 2 (1998): 256.

shaming device serves not only to masculinize the nation (as even the "weakest" among them are exceedingly strong) but also to feminize the empire and its representatives.

In his description of parental love, the author asks, "O, how can I describe the children-loving emotions of parents?" (15:4). Mothers are especially prone to this love: "Mothers become more sympathetic than fathers from their sufferings for those born from them. For the weaker mothers are, the more children they bear, the more they love their children" (15:4b–5). This mother, then, "loved her children more than all mothers," because she is a mother of seven children. Her great love for her children, born out of her "many pangs" (17:7) suffered in childbirth (and thus from her weakness), is set up in contrast to her heroic actions: Even while she suffered during their torture, "pious reason, filling her guts [or womb] with manly courage amidst these passions [τὰ σπλάγχνα αὐτῆς ὁ εὐσεβὴς λογισμὸς ἐν αὐτοῖς τοῖς πάθεσιν ἀνδρειώσας], urged her on to disregard her temporal love for her children" (15:23). This mother was undeterred by her female body and her maternal affection. She overcame her "child-loving emotions [φιλότεκνα γονέων πάθη]" (15:4), encouraging her sons not to transgress the ancestral laws, and then died herself ("some of the guards said that . . . she threw herself into the flames so that no one might touch her body" [17:1]). Her triumph over Antiochus is framed in terms of bravery, a paradigmatically masculine virtue: "because of patient endurance [καρτερίαν], you even conquered [ἐνίκησας] a tyrant, and in deeds and in words you were found more powerful than a man!" (16:14) Though her body is repeatedly portrayed as maternal, and thus female, her victory is framed as powerful and brave, thus male.

Throughout 4 Maccabees, the author compares the mother favorably with Abraham, thus further portraying her as masculine.[239] Although the *Aqedah* is not explicitly described at length, the author repeatedly invokes the example of Abraham.[240] After describing the naturalness of maternal protection, using examples from "even the

---

[239] Abraham is not mentioned in 2 Maccabees 6–7. In *Lamentations Rabbah*, the mother tells her seventh son to address Abraham for her.

[240] Harper Collins NRSV notes that the binding of Isaac is alluded to in 7:14, 13:12, 14:20, 15:28, 16:20, 17:6, and 18:11 (notes to 4 Macc. 13:12, p. 1644).

unreasoning animals" who protect their young (14:14), the author of
4 Maccabees praises the mother: "Sympathy for her children did not
dislodge the mother of the young men, like-souled with Abraham
as she was [τὴν Αβρααμ ὁμόψυχον τῶν νεανίσκων μητέρα]" (14:20; cf.
15:28, 17:6).[241] The mother is consistently portrayed as masculine,
then, and even compared with "father Abraham" (17:6), yet, in her
second speech, the mother emphasizes her proper, feminine attitude
toward her father and her husband: She says, "I was a chaste virgin,
nor did I trespass the boundary of my father's house. . . . I remained
for the time of my prime with a husband" (18:7–8). This speech
serves to domesticate the previously masculine mother; the author
portrays her, in Stephen D. Moore and Janice Capel Anderson's
estimation, as "not unfeminine in relation to her Jewish husband.
She may have mastered the tyrant, but her own master is her husband."[242] As D'Angelo says, "The husband's sudden appearance in
18:9 demotes the mother from teacher of her sons to student of her
husband."[243] Although such assessments seem warranted, given the
"tacked on" nature of the ending, an alternative is to see the ways in
which the author's portrayal of the mother throughout 4 Maccabees
makes her a decidedly queer figure: She is simultaneously a mother
and as courageous as males; she is more manly than the elite man,
but her nonelite (or less elite?) husband is more manly than she. She
embodies the slippage of ancient gender mentioned earlier; although
the narrative hinges on a particular notion of masculinity as bravery
and self-control, the emphasis on this *mother's* manliness shows the
instability of masculinity itself.[244]

---

[241] The text of Sinaiticus calls the mother an "Abrahamite" (Αβρααμιτις) in 18:20; see
DeSilva, *4 Maccabees*, 179.

[242] Moore and Anderson, "Taking It like a Man," 272.

[243] D'Angelo, "*Eusebeia*," 156. DeSilva says D'Angelo "reads with perhaps too sharp
a hermeneutic of suspicion . . . D'Angelo thus seems to be domesticating the author
of 4 Maccabees to the cultural expectations of his period, rather than the author
of 4 Maccabees domesticating the mother with the soul of Abraham" (DeSilva, *4
Maccabees*, 258–59).

[244] Jennifer L. Koosed and Robert Paul Seesengood, "Queer Mothers: Rhetorics of
Gender in Martyrdom" (paper presented at the annual meeting for the Society of
Biblical Literature, Philadelphia, PA, November 2005).

In antiquity, naturalized imagery was closely tied to notions of imitation and similarity. Moreover, the bodies and bodily fluids of one's parents (and wet nurses) were thought to impart certain virtues and tendencies. The boys point to their mother's body as a place of mutual education and instruction (e.g. 10:2, 11:15), and the narrator refers to her body as the origin of the boys and their devotion (13:20–21). Given the importance granted to both the nutritive and moral properties of blood and milk in antiquity (actually the same fluid in different states, according to most ancient gynecologists), this mother represents the biological source of the boys' commitment to divine reason.[245]

The language of "father" and "mother" is crucial in other ways, too. Lieu has argued, "When Razis, who 'risked body and soul for Judaism' and finally committed suicide, is named 'father of the Jews' (2 Macc. 14.37), or when the martyrs are called 'father' or 'mother' (4 Macc. 7.1, 9; 15:29), this is a civic not a familial title," akin to the emperor's use of *pater*.[246] Polycarp is presented as a venerable "father of the Christians" (*Martyrdom of Polycarp* 12:2), and Blandina encourages her co-martyrs "as a noble mother encourages her children" (*Martyrs of Vienne and Lyon*). Lieu is right to see the political implications of naming a martyr "father" or "mother"; this presents them as de facto leaders of the group, as particularly powerful spokespersons, in addition to establishing continuity and a chain of authority. The political import of the title is key, but the biological kinship implications are also relevant because, as Buell says, "martyr narratives presuppose and play on the notion that one's identity is embedded in a multiply inflected social network (that is, gender, status, age, citizenship, language, and ethnicity/race are all salient)"; indeed, familial ties are also relevant.[247] The metaphor of mother/father of the nation works precisely because of the primary biological/kinship meaning, thus implicating biological parenthood in a complex web of meaning related to influence, leadership, power, and continuity of identity.[248] It also serves to naturalize parenthood as a unique role, the only rela-

---

[245] See King, *Hippocrates' Woman*, 143; Glancy, *Corporal Knowledge*, 114; and Aline Rousselle, *Porneia: On Desire and the Body in Antiquity* (New York: Blackwell, 1988), 30.
[246] Lieu, *Image and Reality*, 85.
[247] Buell, *Why This New Race?* 52.
[248] See Buell, *Making Christians*.

tionship that can adequately convey the importance of the maternal/paternal figure in these narratives. This is an especially salient point regarding maternal figures, because these martyrs are leaders precisely as suffering mothers, playing on the apparently "natural" connection between biological maternity and physical pain.

As "mother of the nation [ὦ μήτηρ ἔθνους]" (15:29), the woman who is "like-souled with father Abraham [τὴν Αβρααμ ὁμόψυχον]" (14:20) is an example of Lieu's parental leader. The biological mother of the seven boys is uniquely able to urge them on toward piety; likewise, and by extension, she is uniquely suited to encourage the nation to pious reason as well as to fidelity to ancestral traditions. She proves her worth as a mother/leader by not flinching from her sons' tortures—if she can encourage her own children to remain dedicated to ancestral law, then surely she will do the same for the nation as a whole. In 2 Maccabees, the deaths of these nine figures serve as turning points for the Maccabean revolt as a whole; from their fidelity, the "divine wrath turned to mercy" (8:5; cf. 4 Macc. 18:4). This turning point then hinges on the parental figures; Eleazar and the mother of seven sons as father and mother of the nation lead their compatriots.

Buell has argued, "The popular accounts of early Christian martyrs offer an excellent site for examining how early Christian texts construct a collective identity in which race and religiosity are mutually constituting. . . . In martyr narratives, racial, civic, and national identities are defined not simply through a willingness to suffer but specifically through a willingness to suffer in order to remain pious and maintain religious integrity."[249] Lieu discusses the *Martyrdom of Polycarp*, and Buell presents similar arguments for the *Martyrs of Vienne and Lyon* and the *Acts of the Scillitan Martyrs*; 4 Maccabees, likely earlier than any of those Christian martyrologies, demonstrates a parallel concern for co-constituting racial/civic/national identity with suffering for piety.[250] In a different context, Buell points to the dangers of using maternal metaphors to demonstrate certain religious points, especially when the spiritual/metaphorical image

---

[249] Buell, *Why This New Race?* 53.
[250] Ibid., 52; see also Perkins, *Suffering Self*.

denigrates the experiences of physical mothers.[251] Her caveats are relevant to texts about the Maccabean mother, especially for feminist interpreters thinking about representations and the potential uses of mother-martyrs: What are the consequences for actual mothers when motherhood is connected so strongly and positively to pious suffering for the nation?[252]

Key moments in 4 Maccabees present the reader with pathos and loss; the scene in which the mother witnesses her sons' tortures (15:14–24) emphasizes the carnage and, in Sinaiticus, links the "biological waste matter" of afterbirth with their deaths.[253] A more poignant example comes in 16:5–11, where the narrator tells what the mother's "fainthearted" (16:5) response *could* have been:

> O how wretched am I and many times unhappy! After bearing seven children, I am now the mother of none! O seven childbirths all in vain, seven profitless pregnancies, fruitless nurturings and wretched nursings! In vain, my sons, I endured many birth pangs for you, and the more grievous anxieties of your upbringing. Alas for my children, some unmarried, others married and without offspring. I shall not see your children or have the happiness of being called grandmother. Alas, I who had so many and beautiful children am a widow and alone, with many sorrows. And when I die, I shall have none of my sons to bury me.

Here again, the narrator relies heavily on the physical and biological aspects of mothering: birth (16:6), pregnancy (7), nursing (7), and birth pangs (8). The "cowardly [δειλόψυχος]" (16:5) version of her speech evokes loss of relationships, pain, suffering, and grief, but the author quickly continues, "The holy and God-fearing mother did not bewail any of these with the dirge . . . nor did she grieve as they

---

[251] See Buell, *Making Christians*, 161, 178.
[252] For a foundational text in the larger scholarly conversation about women, gender, and modern nations, see Nira Yuval-Davis, *Gender and Nation* (Thousand Oaks, CA: Sage Publications, 1997).
[253] DeSilva, *4 Maccabees*, 225.

were dying" (16:12). Before narrating the speech she really did give, the author praises her as "mother, soldier of God in piety, elder, and woman! [ὦ μῆτερ δι'εὐσεβείαν θεοῦ... στρατιῶτι πρεσβῦτι καί γύναι]" (16:14). Her words to her sons as they "stood watching Eleazar being tortured" (16:15) are in Hebrew and emphasize the examples of Abraham and Isaac; Daniel; Hananiah, Azariah, and Mishael (20–21). Thus, as she loses her sons to death, she connects them to a larger tradition, looking backward and forward in time.

The encomium to the mother that follows her speech and death (17:1) contains contrasting sentiments (paralleling the contradiction in the idea of martyrdom itself, which celebrates a violent death as a victory and connects death to eternal life): The mother is responsible for "destroying ["nullifying" in NRSV; Greek καταλύσασα] the violence of the tyrant with [her] seven children, rendering his evil intentions void and demonstrating the nobility of faithfulness" (17:2). The willingness of the mother and her sons to die somehow dissipates the tyrant's violence, perhaps because they do not fight back or because they frame death as their victory; their nonresistance neuters Antiochus's violence, just as Antiochus's rage neuters his gender. Moreover, their willingness to die is connected to the nation's survival and continuation. The author compares the mother to the moon, lighting the way of her "star-like seven sons to piety" (17:5). Her guidance and piety result in them all being "firmly fixed" (17:5) in the heavens, just as the moon and stars reside in the sky.

Post-Shoah Context and Jewish Nationalism

The horrors of the Shoah loom large in interpretations of ancient Jewish "martyrdom" narratives.[254] As a recent traumatic event, the Shoah stands out as a rupture in history; though it is, tragically, not the only genocide of the twentieth century, the particular mix of biological racism, theological anti-Judaism, and lethal technological advancements sets the Shoah apart as a distinctly pivotal event,

---

[254] Rajak, "Dying for the Law," 42–43.

in particular for interpreters of early Christianity, early Judaism, and the Bible. Rajak claims that the deaths of Jews in the Holocaust have been universally called martyrdoms; she is right to point to the ways in which mourning, identity, and martyrdom often go together[255]; however, the idea that the six million Jews (and five million others) who died in the Nazi genocide can straightforwardly be called martyrs misses something crucial about earlier kinds of martyrs *and* the Shoah, as Jan Willem van Henten elaborates:

> Many Jewish readers have developed a dislike for the reports of these noble deaths, since associations with the horrible and unnumbered deaths of Jews during the Second World War are obvious. After the Shoah, the attitude of Eleazar the scribe, Razis the elder and the mother with her seven sons— as described in 2 and 4 Maccabees—fills many readers with aversion. . . . The "Maccabean martyrs" do not figure in the modern Israeli collective remembrance of great events in the history of ancient Israel—unlike the Maccabean and Bar Kokhba Revolts, or even the heroic suicide at Masada.[256]

In ancient and medieval narratives, if someone was faced with the choice of maintaining a Jewish identity or dying, "converting," or renouncing Judaism (frequently, the required act was sacrificing to the emperor) could save them. Precisely that choice was lacking in Nazi death camps: Life or death was chosen by the guards, and death for all Jews was, in fact, the goal of the Final Solution.[257] Indeed, in Emil Fackenheim's words, "Hitler murdered Jewish martyrdom itself."[258] Rather than "sanctifying the divine name" by dying as martyrs, some in the camps spoke of "sanctifying life" by surviving.[259] The label "martyr" is thus even more complicated post-Shoah.

---

[255] Rajak, "Dying for the Law," 42–43.
[256] van Henten, *Maccabean Martyrs*, 2.
[257] Shepkaru, *Jewish Martyrs*, 275.
[258] Quoted in ibid.
[259] Leni Yahil, *The Holocaust: The Faith of European Jewry, 1932–1945* (New York: Oxford University Press, 1991), 558.

A further complication rests in the connection between the Shoah and the modern state of Israel. Because the creators of the Jewish state (and Zionist movements pre- and post-Shoah) have claimed certain ancient precedents, the question of how to remember the Maccabean revolt and martyrs is a live one. Boyarin contrasted the value systems associated with Masada and Yavneh, showing how "the events at Masada have become, (in)famously, paradigmatic for a certain modern Jewish consciousness," a consciousness based on masculinized heroism and self-determination.[260] The rabbinic tradition, conversely, locating its origins in Yavneh, "adumbrates an entire— very particular—ethics of colonial survival," one that embodies a stereotyped, feminized stance.[261] Schwartz suggests that the figures in 2 Maccabees 7 embody a "typically diasporan stance" that says, "We are ready to die, not to fight."[262] Post-Shoah and post-1948, the question of Jewish martyrdom (and remembrance of Jewish martyrs) is complicated and painful. This may be even more so the case in considering the Maccabean mother and sons, given that these figures represent a unique position as Jewish martyrs appropriated by later Christians (even, at times, mobilized against the Christians' contemporary Jews).[263]

In addition to considering the Shoah as a crucial historical event that impinges on interpretations of the Maccabean mother, the Israel/Palestine conflict (itself related to the trauma of the Shoah), in conjunction with lingering questions about the continuity of Jewish identity through the centuries, hovers around scholarly work on 4 Maccabees. As considered above, Osiek has noted that the Maccabean mother's willingness to have her sons die (even her encouragement of them to do so) reminds modern readers of a Palestinian mother who expects that "access to glory will be through the death of her

---

[260] Daniel Boyarin, "Masada or Yavneh? Gender and the Arts of Jewish Resistance," in *Jews and Other Differences: The New Jewish Cultural Studies*, ed. Jonathan Boyarin and Daniel Boyarin (Minneapolis: University of Minnesota Press, 1997), 318.
[261] Ibid., 324.
[262] Schwartz, *2 Maccabees*, 301.
[263] See, for example, Joslyn-Siemiatkoski's discussion of Rupert of Deutz (c. 1075–1129 CE) and various leaders in medieval Cologne in his *Christian Memories of the Maccabean Martyrs*, 87, 143–44, 154.

sons."[264] In Osiek's interpretation, this mother could just as easily be part of the Second Intifada as part of the Maccabean revolt, as she nationalizes and politicizes the violent deaths of her children. Streete, however, highlights the crucial distinction between the Maccabean mother, on the one hand, and a suicide bomber, on the other: While one accepts death and encourages her children to die, the other kills her enemies in her own suicide.[265] Readers might also think of Israelis who move their families to settlements in violation of international law; in doing so, they willingly endanger their children's lives because of their commitment to a certain strand of Zionist thought.[266]

Although no direct line links the Maccabean mother to either a Jewish-settlement mother or a Palestinian suicide bomber's mother, modern audiences remain haunted by the connections, even if the analogs are imperfect. Osiek and Streete's comparisons with Palestinian mothers show that even mothers who might seem utterly opposed to Jewish mothers have remarkable similarities with the Maccabean mother. Thus, we might recognize her as a maternal figure being mobilized as propaganda for a particular nationalist/religious cause, which is elaborated in connection with specific religio-philosophical commitments. Maternal figures are especially useful in those endeavors because in the maternal body, pain and endurance are linked with fruitful reproduction, in addition to symbolizing the continuity and transmission of a tradition.

---

[264] Osiek, "*Pietas* in and out of the Frying Pan," 169. Here, Osiek is referring specifically to 2 Maccabees 7.

[265] Streete, *Redeemed Bodies*, 103–22.

[266] Jeffrey Goldberg, "Among the Settlers," *New Yorker*, May 31, 2004, http://www.newyorker.com/magazine/2004/05/31/among-the-settlers. Goldberg calls this a Moriah complex, which he describes as "a desire to match Abraham's devotion to God, even at the price of a child's life." His discussion references not only Abraham's near-sacrifice of Isaac on Mount Moriah but also the Maccabean mother traditions.

CHAPTER 4

Mother Martyrs: Perpetua, Felicitas, and Their Infants

L ike the many later narratives about Mary and the Maccabean mother, the various retellings of the *Passion of Perpetua and Felicitas* indicate the ways in which audiences and interpreters through the centuries have used these two mother-martyrs to reflect on familial expectations, religious commitments, and gender roles. Although the afterlives of these narratives are not quite as vivid and varied as those of the Maccabean mother or Mary, there are a few key retellings of the *Passion* (c. 203 CE): *The Acts of Perpetua and Felicitas* (c. 260 CE);[267] *The Golden Legend* (which also includes the narrative about Felicitas of Rome and her seven sons); and some late antique homilies, including Augustine's.[268] In each case, the women are considered heroic when they relinquish their family ties to embrace martyrs' deaths in the arena. This willingness to die while leaving their young children and others behind is a narrative device meant to surprise and horrify audiences; the reaction of modern scholars indicates that the

---

[267] The *Passion* (extant in Greek and Latin) is generally considered to be earlier than the *Acts* (extant only in Latin, but in two distinct versions). Previously, the *Acts* were dated to the fifth century CE, but Jan Bremmer's recent work has argued for a date "shortly after AD 260." For his discussion, see Jan N. Bremmer, "Felicitas: The Martyrdom of a Young African Woman," in *Perpetua's Passions: Multidisciplinary Approaches to the Passio Perpetuae et Felicitatis*, ed. Jan N. Bremmer and Marco Formisano (New York: Oxford University Press, 2012), 38–40; for arguments about the older, fifth-century CE dating, see J. W. Halporn, "Literary History and Generic Expectations in the *Passio* and *Acta Perpetuae*," *Vigiliae Christianae* 45, no. 3 (September 1991): 225.

[268] Sermons 280–282 commemorate Perpetua and Felicitas; see Augustine, *Sermons 273–305A (III/8)*, trans. Edmund Hill, O.P. (Hyde Park, NY: New City Press, 1994), 72–82. Tertullian also mentions them in *On the Soul* 55.4.

device remains effective. Many have expressed disappointment and disbelief at Perpetua and Felicitas's actions (much as the audience in the arena does): How could mothers with young babies (both still nursing, one a newborn) leave their children when they are clearly given chances to live?

My interpretation here emphasizes the communal aspects of this narrative; it seems clear that one could focus on both Perpetua and Felicitas, in addition to the other catechumens, Revocatus, Saturninus, and Secundulus, but many interpreters remain hyperfocused on Perpetua, mentioning other characters (her father, her baby, Felicitas) as supporting roles in *her* drama. The inclusion of her purported prison diary, especially because it is a substantial part of the text and falls in the middle, sets the audience up to be most concerned about Perpetua and to see her perspective, but even much of her diary focuses on her relationships with other people (her brother, her baby, her father, and so on). By focusing on other figures in the text (especially Felicitas, the other eponymous mother-martyr), I highlight the ways in which this text connects maternity to a larger horizon of concern than one's biological family. The devotion and commitment that Perpetua and Felicitas show to the Christian family of co-martyrs (while also displaying concern for their own biological relatives, especially children) contrasts strongly with certain scholarly interpretations of these figures, which sometimes emphasize the women's callous, detached attitudes.

The Narrative of the Passion

Scholars often divide the *Passion of Perpetua and Felicitas* by author. The text begins in the voice of an editor who connects the events of the *Passion* to Joel's prophecy: "Then afterward, I will pour out my spirit on all flesh; your sons and your daughters shall prophesy, your old men shall dream dreams, and your young men shall see visions. Even on the male and female slaves, in those days, I will pour out my spirit" (Joel 2:28–29; Acts 2:16–18; *PPF* 1.4). The editor of the *Passion* makes a case for valuing new visions and prophecies in addition to ancient ones: "If ancient examples of faith that attest the grace of God and cause the edification of man have been written down so that God may be glorified and man strengthened when those deeds are read aloud—by making those deeds, as it were, visibly present—then why should new documents not also be published that likewise serve either end?" (1.1).[269] Then, the editor adds another reason: Even the newer documents will eventually be ancient and thus more valuable (1.2)—and so he introduces a new example of faith, describing the arrest of Revocatus and Felicitas, "his fellow slave" (2.1), Saturninus and Secundulus, and Vibia Perpetua. He describes the twenty-two-year-old Perpetua more than the other catechumens; she was "well born, well educated, honorably married [*honeste nata, liberaliter instituta, matronaliter nupta*], and . . . had a father, a mother, and two brothers, one of them also a catechumen, and an infant son at her breast" (2.2).

Then the voice of the text switches to the prison diary: "Now from this point on the entire account of her ordeal is her own, according to her own ideas and in the way that she herself wrote it down" (*PPF* 2.3). In chapters 3–10, Perpetua details her tense relationship with her father, her experiences in prison with the other catechumens, and her visions, which she narrates. In all, she has four encounters with her distraught father, as well as four visions; her father continually tries to dissuade her from calling herself a Christian. She refuses, first by giving the example of a "vase" or "pitcher" [*vas . . . urceolum*], which cannot be called by any other name, just as she can only call herself a Christian (3.1–2). In later chapters, her father begs her, "Have pity on my grey head, have pity on me, your father" (5.2) and "Perform the sacrifice—have pity on your baby [*Supplica. Miserere infanti*]!" (6.2). Perpetua's description of their last encounter, in chapter 9, includes no dialogue but describes her father's sorrow and desperation: He plucks out parts of his beard and throws them to the ground, "saying the kinds of things that would move the whole of creation" (9.2).

Her accounts of her four visions are even more vivid. The first, in chapter 4, includes a ladder stretching into the heavens with a dragon

---

[269] I relied on the translation by Joseph Farrell and Craig Williams, published in Bremmer and Formisano, *Perpetua's Passions*, 14–24. I have also compared with Herbert Musurillo, *The Acts of the Christian Martyrs* (Oxford: Clarendon, 1972).

waiting at its bottom. She steps on the dragon's head and climbs the ladder to the top, where she meets a shepherd in a garden who calls her "child" and gives her some cheese to eat. When she wakes up, she is still chewing on something sweet and realizes "we would suffer and at that point we gave up our hopes for this world" (4.10). The second and third visions happen in quick succession, and both concern her dead brother, Dinocrates. In chapter 7, she calls his name in prayer quite unexpectedly and is granted a vision in which she sees her brother, who died from facial cancer at age seven. He is hot and thirsty, but unable to reach the basin of water because he is too short. After this vision, she prays for him and receives another vision: "I see the same spot that I had seen before, but there was Dinocrates all clean, well dressed, and refreshed" (8.1). He was able to drink from the basin, and then he "began playing in the water the way little children do, gleefully" (8.4). From this vision, she realizes her prayers released her dead brother from his suffering. Her fourth and final vision, which includes a bout with an Egyptian gladiator in the arena, is the last part of her diary. She describes being undressed by attendants after entering the amphitheater, and then changing into a man: *et expoliata sum et facta sum masculus* (10.7). She defeats the gladiator and is given a green branch with golden apples; after this vision, she realizes "that it was not with wild animals that I would fight but with the Devil, but I knew that I would win the victory" (10.14).

The voice switches again in chapters 11–13 to her co-martyr Saturus, who also gives an account of his heavenly vision while in prison, a vision in which Perpetua also appears. Then the editor, presumably the same voice that introduced Perpetua's diary at the beginning of the text, concludes with a vivid account of the martyrs' deaths in the arena (chapters 14–21). He begins by describing Felicitas, for she also is touched by "the Lord's favor" (15.1). Pregnant when they were arrested, she is now in her eighth month and is afraid she will be unable to enter the arena with her fellow catechumens, "for it is against the law for women with child to be executed" (15.2). She and her fellow catechumens pray for her, and she gives birth prematurely to a daughter, who is given to another member of the Christian community. Two days later, the catechumens leave the prison and enter the amphitheater "cheerfully, as if going to heaven" (18.1), and the editor describes the two women: Perpetua looks like "the wife of Christ, the beloved of God [*matrona Christi, ut Dei delicata*], parrying the gaze of all with the strength of her own" (18.2), and Felicitas, who is glad to have given birth, goes "from one blood bath to another, from the midwife to the gladiator [*a sanguine ad sanguinem, ab obstetrice ad retiarium*], to wash after childbirth in her second baptism" (18.3). In the arena, a mad heifer "was chosen that their sex might be matched with that of the beast" (20.1) and the women are stripped and placed in nets to face the cow. But the crowd is horrified at the sight of the two naked women, "one a delicate girl, the other fresh from childbirth with milk dripping from her breasts" (20.2), so Perpetua and Felicitas are clothed again and sent back into the arena. In the end, their throats are cut, although Perpetua has to guide the "trembling hand of the young gladiator . . . as though so great a woman . . . could not be dispatched unless she herself were willing" (21.9–10). The editor then concludes with an encomium to the "brave and blessed martyrs" and reminds the audience that these "new deeds of bravery" (21.11), in addition the old, are significant for the edification of the church.

Interpretive Issues: Maternal Care

A central assumption for many scholars is that the *Passion of Perpetua and Felicitas* reflects "real" events and thus that Perpetua's diary gives us unfettered access to an ancient woman's inner life.[270] Danuta Shanzer provides a typical assessment characteristic of this approach:

> This extraordinary and moving text preserves at its heart
> the first preserved autobiographical account written by an
> ancient woman. No other single text can convey as vivid

---

[270] See, for example, Maureen Tilley, "The Passion of Perpetua and Felicity," in Schüssler Fiorenza, *Searching the Scriptures*, 831; and Jan Willem van Henten, "Jewish and Christian Martyrs," in *Saints and Role Models in Judaism and Christianity*, ed. Joshua Schwartz and Marcel Poorthuis (Boston: Brill, 2004), 171.

an impression of the impact of an imperial persecution upon the individual, from arrest, to courtroom, to prison, to execution in the amphitheatre. This text also provides wonderful material on the dreams of the martyrs and their expectations and fears of death and the afterlife.[271]

Brent Shaw's work on Perpetua (which, like much of the scholarship about this text, does not focus on Felicitas) similarly highlights the liberating and empowering potential of a "real" ancient woman's diary. His historical assumptions related to facticity are problematic, especially given his larger argument that the prison diary itself is authentic and "unmediated" and the text includes a "male editor's additions."[272] He argues, "Establishing the primacy of what Perpetua experienced, thought, saw and felt is not only a rare possibility granted to the historian, but also demands that we reproduce a faithful version of how she saw herself and the ways in which she interpreted what was happening to her."[273]

Although Shaw and other interpreters assume that Perpetua's diary represents an authentic woman's writing from antiquity, Judith Perkins, writing nearly fifteen years after Shaw, has challenged this assumption. About Perpetua and Felicitas, she writes, "Their depictions are so rhetorically pertinent to the discourse of the period in Carthage as evidenced by Tertullian as to make suspect the women's authenticity as real persons. Their representations seem to coincide too closely with the theological polemics of the period not to have been crafted to fit a specific historical argument."[274] She further notes,

---

[271] Danuta Shanzer, "Literature, History, Periodization, and the Pleasures of the Latin Literary History of Late Antiquity," *History Compass* 7, no. 3 (2009): 917–54, quotation on p. 934.

[272] Brent D. Shaw, "The Passion of Perpetua," *Past and Present*, no. 139 (May 1993): 20. Reprinted as Brent D. Shaw, "The Passion of Perpetua," in *Studies in Ancient Greek and Roman Society*, ed. Robin Osborne (New York: Cambridge University Press, 2004), 286–325, with a brief postscript.

[273] Shaw, "Passion of Perpetua," *Studies in Ancient Greek and Roman Society*, 301.

[274] Judith Perkins, "The Rhetoric of the Maternal Body in the Passion of Perpetua," in *Mapping Gender in Ancient Religious Discourse*, ed. Todd Penner and Caroline Vander Stichele (Boston: Brill, 2007), 316, reprinted in Judith Perkins, *Roman Imperial Identities in the Early Christian Era* (London: Routledge, 2009), 159–71.

"The loss of Perpetua's testimony as a historical figure will diminish women's history. Her function in this narrative, however, which is to figure the imperative of the vulnerable body's call to interdependence and ethical responsibility, has important implications for the lives of both men and women."[275] The assumption that the diary gives interpreters access to what Perpetua "experienced, thought, saw and felt" is not guaranteed, but, as Perkins argues, it gives other kinds of historical information, even if not about the "historical Perpetua."[276]

A number of scholars have joined with Perkins to question a straightforward assumption of the historical role of Perpetua in authoring any part of this text.[277] Instead of asking about the "real" Perpetua (or Felicitas, often occluded in these historicity debates[278]; see below), I follow Perkins's lead in focusing on the function of the text's rhetoric, especially the ways in which the text constructs each mother-martyr and maternity and the kinds of legacies or memories that the text engenders: Christianness, state terror, familial ties, pain/violence, and group solidarity. Perkins's approach, then, is a way of asking historical questions but not specifically about the historical Perpetua.

Many modern interpretations of the *Passion of Perpetua and Felicitas* focus on gender in addition to historicity, not only because the two eponymous martyrs are women (and women are often marked as gendered in a way that men are not) but also because of Perpetua's unstable, shifting gender. Like the Maccabean mother, she is a female character with striking masculine characteristics. Certain

---

[275] Perkins, "Rhetoric of the Maternal Body," 316n12. This is a reversal of her earlier stance; see her *The Suffering Self: Pain and Narrative Representation in the Early Christian Era* (New York: Routledge, 1995), 104, in which she says it "is an extraordinary document, for the narrator, by including Perpetua's first-person record of her imprisonment, preserves for us the clearest woman's voice (except, perhaps, Sappho's) to speak from the ancient world."

[276] Shaw, "Passion of Perpetua," 301.

[277] Ross Kraemer, "When Is a Text about a Woman a Text about a Woman? The Cases of Aseneth and Perpetua," in *A Feminist Companion to Patristic Literature*, ed. Amy-Jill Levine and Maria Mayo Robbins (London: T & T Clark, 2008), 156–72.

[278] But see Perkins, who says in her "Rhetoric of the Maternal Body" (330–31) that Felicitas is less likely to be authentic than Perpetua is; see also Ross Shepard Kraemer, *Unreliable Witnesses: Religion, Gender, and History in the Greco-Roman Mediterranean* (New York: Oxford University Press, 2011), 244.

features in the text emphasize her femininity and/or femaleness: She is a "matron" (2.1) who has "an infant son at the breast" (2.2) and is addressed as "Daughter" (5.2, 10.13) and "Lady, sister" (4.1). In the arena, the crowd is shocked that she is "delicate" (20.2) and honorable, covering her thighs (20.4) and pinning back her hair (20.5) in order to preserve her modesty and decorum. And yet a key moment in her fourth vision disrupts the easy connection between Perpetua and femininity/femaleness: As she prepared to face an Egyptian in the arena, she says, "My clothes were stripped off, and suddenly I was a man [*et expoliata sum et facta sum masculus*]" (10.7). Other moments in the narrative present her in a masculinized fashion: She displays self-control when she rhetorically "defeats" her father, as well as bravery as she enters the arena to face her death.[279] The dream transformation more than any other feature of the text, however, is crucial for interpreters who discuss the importance of gender in this text, especially Perpetua's gender.

In her study of Perpetua (as part of a larger work focused on the productive possibilities of shame), Virginia Burrus notes that "at the center of this complexly polyglossal text is the spectacle of a young woman's repeatedly exposed body"—a body that, we are constantly reminded, retains its maternal markings, even though Perpetua "became a man" in one of her dreams.[280] These repeatedly exposed maternal bodies (Felicitas's maternal body is also a focus) induce shock and surprise when they are exposed in the arena: "So they were stripped naked, placed in nets and thus brought out into the arena. Even the crowd was horrified when they saw that one was a delicate young girl [*puellam delicatam*] and the other was a woman fresh from child birth with the milk still dripping from her breasts [*a partu recentem stillantibus mammis*]" (20.2). The continued exposure of these bodies is a consistent reminder of their gender—and they are gendered especially related to their motherhood.

Gail Streete's work focuses on the ways in which religious ideas— here, martyrdom—are "so often written on bodies, particularly those

---

[279] L. Stephanie Cobb, *Dying to Be Men: Gender and Language in Early Christian Martyr Texts* (New York: Columbia University Press, 2008), 94–111.
[280] Burrus, *Saving Shame*, 28.

of women."[281] She also focuses on the legacy of religious violence, especially as it concerns women, in a way that critiques religious truths "accomplished over the dead bodies of women, most of them young."[282] Perkins's work on the *Passion of Perpetua and Felicitas* has similarly focused on the ways in which the vulnerable, tortured body is used theologically, philosophically, and rhetorically.[283] Perkins makes a compelling case that the *Passion of Perpetua and Felicitas* presents the vulnerable body as the real human universal, experienced by all, and that this approach could have "offered an opening that, if it had been pursued, would have gone far to assuage the violence that many maintain is the real 'universal,' the recurring traumatic kernel, at the center of every human society."[284] Perkins shows that the maternal body, here presented in explicitly maternal situations (birthing, nursing), is given as a paradigm of humanity at its most "disgusting," its most "animal."[285] By focusing on the maternal body as potentially useful for assuaging violence rather than causing it, Perkins's approach offers a counterpoint to Streete's arguments.[286]

Even though both women are catechumens and mothers, interpreters often note (at least in passing) the status differences between the slave woman (Felicitas) and the freeborn *matrona* (Perpetua). Sometimes, interpreters question whether Felicitas was Perpetua's slave; other times, they assume it to be true.[287] Nevertheless, many interpreters posit (or declare!) that Perpetua and Felicitas experienced

---

[281] Streete, *Redeemed Bodies*, x.

[282] Ibid., 111.

[283] Perkins, *Suffering Self* and "Rhetoric of the Maternal Body."

[284] Perkins, "Rhetoric of the Maternal Body," 314.

[285] Ibid., 160, 163. In this way, Perkins says, the *Passion of Perpetua and Felicitas* is strikingly similar to Tertullian's work on the resurrection, nativity, and crucifixion, as he emphasizes the corporality of Jesus (and of Mary, as the "source" of Jesus), against the teachings of Marcion.

[286] Laura Copier's discussion of Julia Kristeva's theory of the abject and the maternal has resonances with Perkins's argument (see Laura Copier, "Maternal Martyrdom: *Alien3* and the Power of the Female Martyr," in *Powers: Religion as a Social and Spiritual Force*, ed. Meerten B. ter Borg and Jan Willem van Henten [New York: Oxford University Press, 2010], 275–91).

[287] Musurillo calls Felicitas Perpetua's "personal slave-girl" in his introduction to the text (see *Acts of the Christian Martyrs*, xxvi). Keith Bradley says this is probable ("Sacrificing the Family: Christian Martyrs and Their Kin," *Ancient Narrative* 3 [2003]: 167).

a close relationship, beginning either in prison or in the arena, that demonstrates the apparent power of Christian identity to overcome social barriers such as status. Sara Parvis's assessment is typical:

> A maddened cow tossed the two of them around, but Perpetua sits up, fixes her dress, fixes her hair, gets up and goes and lifts up Felicity, and stands with her hand in hand in the middle of the arena (20.6). And in that gesture her theology of the family of God is most perfectly encapsulated. The young *matrona*, well born, and liberally educated, who chose to throw her lot in with slaves and criminals and be their mother and sister and daughter, is to be brought down by the Roman judicial and gubernatorial system, as a class traitor and a family traitor, and made an example of. But she brings the judicial system down, and brings her companions up, lifting Felicity from the dust to stand beside her, undefeated, *matrona* and slave together. And thus they defeat the crowd too, whose harshness is overcome, so they are called over to the Sanavivarian Gate— the gate to the amphitheatre known locally as the "gate of health and life" (20.7).[288]

Other scholars see similar evidence for solidarity and in-group relationship, which may indicate a desire for ancient and modern Christianity to be a religious system that uniquely transcends such social boundaries and renders a slave's hardships benign (or spiritualizes them as hardships to be endured with God's help). Moreover, it may represent a desire for contemporary mothers to have similar experiences and to share similar political and social positions based on their maternity; that is, motherhood is essentialized as such a constitutive and crucial part of a woman's identity that it makes mothers a unified political entity. In a similar way, Jennifer Glancy, like Parvis, argues that, at the level of the text,

---

[288] Sara Parvis, "Perpetua," *Expository Times* 120, no. 8 (May 2009): 365–72, quotation on 371.

Pregnancy, childbirth, and lactation were among the
somatic experiences that potentially linked slave and free
women. . . . Perpetua's own words stressed the primacy
of the experiences of lactation and weaning for a woman
awaiting death. The editor who added the account of the
martyrs' deaths in the arena equally stressed the effect that
Felicity's lactation had on the crowd that witnessed her
death. In at least one bloody context, the capacity to produce milk dissolved differences between an elite woman
and a humble slave woman.[289]

Glancy does not seem to be arguing about the historical figures and
their feelings or motivations, as some other interpreters do; she
instead focuses on the effect of the editor's presentation. Rather than
attributing the women's solidarity to their shared commitment to
Christian ideals about the "family of God" as Parvis does, Glancy
emphasizes their shared experience as mothers.

John Marshall helpfully, though briefly, reminds interpreters to
consider both gender and class in their interpretations of Perpetua
and Felicitas; it will not do to point to the apparent gender solidarity
between Perpetua and Felicitas when they are separated so starkly by
class, he says. Marshall seems especially to be pushing back against
the frequent claims made about what "must have happened" between
women in the early church.[290] Marshall, accepting the claims of
authenticity in the text, highlights an apparent oversight in Perpetua's
diary: "Perpetua, for her part, writes an intensely relational text focusing on her father and brothers, mentioning by name fellow martyr
Saturnus and the deacons Pomponius and Tertius. Felicitas, the slave
and other woman in the group, who, according to the narrative, gave

---

[289] Jennifer A. Glancy, *Slavery in Early Christianity* (New York: Oxford University Press,
2002), 17.
[290] See, for example, Carolyn Osiek and Margaret Y. MacDonald, *A Woman's Place:
House Churches in Earliest Christianity* (Minneapolis, MN: Fortress, 2006), 19, in which
they suggest, "We must keep in mind the existence of a world of women about which
the texts remain silent—a world of sisterhood, conversation, and exchange among
women on issues of hospitality, childcare, service, and allegiance to Christ under the
authority of a (sometimes pagan) *paterfamilias* as a wife, daughter, or slave, a world
where distinctions among various categories of women possibly broke down."

birth in prison and would share so many of the concerns that Perpetua foregrounds in her discussions of the fate of her own infant son, is not mentioned at all."[291] Many interpreters tend to assume solidarity between the two women, without acknowledging, as Marshall does, that class/status may have still remained an insurmountable barrier between these two figures.[292] Although certain textual moments indicate the women's shared experience (like Perpetua helping Felicitas in the arena in 20.6, cited by Parvis above), Marshall's emphasis on their significant status differences and Perpetua's occlusion of Felicitas in her prison diary enables interpreters to recognize the possible effects of ancient slave systems on both ancient women and the construction of ancient texts.

Attention to the rhetoric of family and household is a crucial element of scholarship on the *Passion of Perpetua and Felicitas*; not only are family language and household structures important features of this text in particular, but the impact of such language, structures, and norms in the ancient world cannot be underestimated. When scholars make claims about ancient families like Perpetua's, including what the ancients may or may not have felt about their families, they are also frequently moralizing about what is normal, natural, and expected in families—including modern families—throughout time. Although recent scholarship on the ancient household highlights the lives and roles of women, slaves, and children, who are often occluded in ancient texts and historical scholarship, attending to the rhetorical work of "the family" in both ancient and scholarly texts draws attention to the stakes of such constructs. Moreover, a focus on maternal figures necessarily implies a concern for children, but this focus is typically performed glibly rather than in a nuanced,

---

[291] John W. Marshall, "Postcolonialism and the Practice of History," in *Her Master's Tools? Feminist and Postcolonial Engagements of Historical-Critical Discourse*, ed. Caroline Vander Stichele and Todd C. Penner (Leiden: Brill, 2005), 102. Marshall compares this to Spivak's essay that focuses on the role of Bertha Mason as Jane Eyre's counterpoint.

[292] Osiek and MacDonald acknowledge that "in most slave systems, while slaves undeniably have sex, they do not have gender . . . [a slave woman could not] claim any status privileges in the cultural construct of womanhood" (Osiek and MacDonald, *A Woman's Place*, 96); see also Sandra R. Joshel and Sheila Murnaghan, eds., *Women and Slaves in Greco-Roman Culture: Differential Equations* (New York: Routledge, 1998).

critical way. Keith Bradley, for example, whose work on family and children in ancient Rome is influential, describes Felicitas:

> In Felicitas' Christian view of the world, her child's birth was inconsequential in comparison with the anticipated glory of martyrdom, a view that once more illustrates how Christian ideology could bring about a total inversion of the natural order.[293] When her child was born prematurely it was of course a miracle, an answer to prayer from her fellow prisoners that allowed her execution to proceed on schedule—the infant herself, orphaned virtually at birth, being entrusted to a Christian woman who, naturally enough, was a "sister." Thus it was that the mother went to her death, *rejoicing*. . . . A greater perversion of nature it is difficult to imagine.[294]

Bradley's arguments about what a family "naturally" is and how mothers "naturally" feel or act toward their children are not unusual; many scholars describe Perpetua and Felicitas as acting against their maternal nature. Although little scholarship on the *Passion of Perpetua and Felicitas* to date has taken into account recent work done in the study of ancient childhood, this growing interdisciplinary field should figure in future scholarly assessments of children's needs and motherly duty in antiquity. A particularly pressing problem is the tendency for modern interpreters to assume that children need biological mothers as their primary caregivers (a post-Freudian obsession); this assumption in a world populated with wet nurses and pedagogues is problematic.

For many interpreters, the Maccabean mother is strikingly different from Perpetua and Felicitas: As one who encourages her children to die and who dies alongside them (contrasted with Perpetua and Felicitas who give their babies to others so they themselves can die),

---

[293] He describes Agathonice in a similar way: "an unnatural mother whose actions to the non-Christian majority are incomprehensible. To Christians, frighteningly, she is an example of courage and commitment" (Bradley, "Sacrificing the Family," 161).
[294] Ibid., 172.

she seems to avoid a familial rupture that they do not. Jan Willem
van Henten focuses on the motif of motherly love (so prevalent in
4 Maccabees but entirely missing in the *Passion*), concluding that
"the Maccabean martyrdoms describe how the mother and her sons
die together in solidarity on the same day, but the *Passion* implies
that it is impossible to be a mother and a martyr at the same time.
The transition of Perpetua and Felicitas to the household of Christ
terminate their biological family relations."[295] Bradley likewise sees
dissimilarity between the two texts: "There is no familial discord"
for the mother of the Maccabees, while the first part of Perpetua's
diary focuses intently on her increasing distance and independence
from her father and infant son.[296] While Bradley concedes that it may
be surprising to think of Christians as undermining the traditional
family, his argument rests on a reading of martyrdom texts that sees
Christians as promoting family discord in a way unprecedented in
Roman history before the Christian period.[297] By easily equating one's
biological family with one's "real" family (see, for example, Bradley's
description of the "new, artificial Christian family"), scholars implicitly define what family "really" is and what one's responsibilities
toward that family are.[298] Moreover, historiographical assumptions
about how martyr texts are related to historical events (and the
effects of such texts on ancient audiences) assume that martyr texts
give us windows to ancient realities. Reading martyr texts as simply
giving information about historical events misses the rhetorical and
didactic purposes of such texts, in addition to overlooking the ways
in which historical memory works. The desire to see Christianity as
generating family conflicts and disruptions in an unnatural, unprecedented way does not allow interpreters to acknowledge the ways in
which Christian martyr texts, just like other texts of this period, were

---

[295] Jan Willem van Henten, "The *Passio Perpetuae* and Jewish Martyrdom: The Motif
of Motherly Love," in Bremmer and Formisano, *Perpetua's Passions*, 133. Van Henten
compares both ancient texts with the film *Alien 3*, as does Copier in "Maternal
Martyrdom."

[296] Bradley, "Sacrificing the Family," 155n7.

[297] Ibid., 152–53.

[298] Ibid., 160.

wrestling with issues of changing family norms, the threat of imperial violence, and gendered expectations.

Mary Lefkowitz's well-known 1976 article, a "psycho-historical analysis" of Perpetua, is apparently the first to pursue the line of argumentation that traditional family patterns in the Roman Empire were oppressive to women and that Perpetua (along with other women martyrs) was able to seek freedom from this oppression by joining a new religious movement and demonstrating her willingness to die for that cause.[299] Lefkowitz calls this an "abnormal, extreme form of social protest. . . . Modern anthropologists would compare it to the sudden ecstatic experiences that bring oppressed groups a sense (albeit transient) of political power."[300] There is a way in which this approach (pursued by others since) displays both a familiarity and an incredulity with the idea of maternal martyrdom: It is thinkable that a woman would feel oppressed and do something extreme, but it is also nearly unthinkable that a woman would willingly accept death and estrangement from her family, especially her (young) child. Often without acknowledging it, these kinds of scholarly arguments are deeply imbedded in modern conversations about women and family. Lefkowitz's article, for example, was published in 1976, just a year before Adrienne Rich's *Of Woman Born*, which famously made the distinction between mothering as an institution (which is inherently oppressive) and mothering as an experience (which many find enjoyable and life-giving). Lefkowitz seems to have been wrestling with similar tensions, as she affirms the oppression that early Christian women experienced in their families but also admits surprise at their actions.

Punk Protests: The (Maternal) Activism of Pussy Riot

The protests and subsequent trial of Pussy Riot, a Russian feminist art collective, evoke the tension between communal concerns and motherhood, which is so often understood as a privatized

---

[299] Mary R. Lefkowitz, "Motivations for St. Perpetua's Martyrdom," *Journal of the American Academy of Religion* 44, no. 3 (Summer 1976): 417.
[300] Ibid., 419.

role. The women of Pussy Riot staged a public protest in Moscow's Cathedral of Christ the Savior on February 21, 2012, just weeks before the Russian election that year.[301] Their brief performance art included thirty seconds of genuflecting and crossing themselves at the altar, wearing short skirts and balaclavas, and singing the lyrics, "Mother Mary, drive away Putin." Days later, a YouTube version of the performance went viral; it included a full song entitled "Punk Prayer" and footage of their protest in the cathedral. The song implores the Virgin Mother to become a feminist and join them in protest; it also samples from Rachmaninov's *Ave Maria*. Three of the members of the group, Nadezhda Tolokonnikova, Maria Alyokhina, and Yekaterina Samutsevich, were arrested and tried on charges of "hooliganism motivated by religious hatred"; after six months of testimony, they were sentenced to two years in a labor camp (a sentence that seems to have been a foregone conclusion, even though Vladimir Putin publicly asked for the court to show mercy and the Russian Orthodox Church hierarchy officially extended forgiveness to the women). Tolokonnikova and Alyokhina had preschool-aged children at home; they not only risked their own freedom but did so knowing that they could miss years with their young children.[302] When supporters of the group rallied for their freedom, one of their daughters often held a sign that said, "Free my mommy!" All three have since been released from prison.

In their noteworthy closing statements, the women of Pussy Riot gave apologias on behalf of their group and grand traditions of social dissidence in general. They located their protest in a line stretching from Socrates to Stephen the Martyr to Dostoevsky and the Russian poets of OBERIU (or Union of Real Art), known for their absurdist public performances in the early twentieth century. They refused to address the actual charges because "it's not the three Pussy Riot

---

[301] Masha Gessen, *Words Will Break Cement: The Passion of Pussy Riot* (New York: Riverhead, 2014). Gessen has been a persistent voice for acknowledging Donald J. Trump as an autocrat in the wake of the 2016 US elections. The activism of Pussy Riot thus takes on a heightened relevance for readers in the United States, given the growing evidence of a Putin–Trump alliance.

[302] Mary Elizabeth Williams, "Pussy Riot's Victorious Defeat," *Salon*, August 17, 2012, http://www.salon.com/2012/08/17/pussy_riots_victorious_defeat/.

singers who are on trial here. If it were, what happens here would
be of no consequence whatsoever. But it is the entire Russian state
system that is on trial here" and the world's verdict had already been
announced.[303] Despite appearances, Tolokonnikova emphasized,
"We have more freedom than the people who are sitting opposite
us, on the side of the accusers, because we can say what we want
and we do say what we want. Whereas the people over there [Nadya
pointed at the prosecutor], they say only that which political censor-
ship allows them to say. They cannot say the words '"Mother of God,
chase Putin out," a punk prayer.' . . . Their mouths are sewn shut."[304]
The speeches are peppered with biblical references both explicit and
implicit, especially related to truth, persecution for righteousness's
sake, and freedom. Their statements reject the terms of their arrest,
imprisonment, and trial as unjust and, ultimately, impotent: Even
though the court condemns them, they remain undeterred and committed to their core values. Moreover, they demonstrate that the trial
and media attention emboldened the women to brave speech, even
given the threat of real punishment.

Eliot Borenstein, a scholar of Russian and Slavic studies,
explored the various implications of the name "Pussy Riot," showing that although it is a bold, potentially offensive English phrase,
it remains incomprehensible (and nearly unpronounceable) to
Russian speakers.[305] Moreover, it shows the group's debt to French
feminism, as it explicitly locates resistance and agency in the female
body. "Pussy," as the counterpoint of the insults "cock" and "dick,"
recasts normative power dynamics as it resists appropriating phallic
discourses of power and effectiveness; instead of imagining a riot that
is forceful or violent, this group's riot is more like a trap. The name
also locates power in the ability to say no to male agency. Borenstein
noted that Russian media portrayals of this case sometimes focused
on the women's motherhood: At times, the media expressed sur-

---

[303] Quoted in Gessen, *Words Will Break Cement*, 195. Other translators have used
the written speeches as sources for their translations, but Gessen has translated the
speeches as they were spoken aloud during the trial.
[304] Quoted in ibid., 199, 200 (brackets in original).
[305] Eliot Borenstein, "Pussy Riot: Performing Scandal in Putin's Russia" (paper presented at Drew University, March 5, 2013).

prise that the two young mothers were willing to miss years of their
children's lives in order to participate in performance art to protest
Putin; moreover, Tolokonnikova had participated in a group sex act
in the Biology Museum in Moscow when she was heavily pregnant,
as part of an earlier protest through the group Voina. Non-Russian
media focused on the women's motherhood less frequently but
still noted the apparent tension between motherhood and activism.
For example, in a *60 Minutes* segment, reporter Leslie Stahl asked
Pyotr Verzilov, Tolokonnikova's husband, "Did you and Nadia talk
about your child and the consequences? I'm talking about before-
hand, the consequences of this little girl being raised without her
mother." Verzilov answered, "Well, obviously we did talk about that
enormously. But if you really want to change history, you have to be
able to put everything you have on the line, and then you do have a
chance of changing it. I mean, changing history is not a hobby. It's
not something you can take part-time."[306] In various media portrayals, especially in Russia, the mothers appeared callous to their young
children's needs and lives; the Russian government, however, ended
up looking worse. Russian laws allow women to wait until their children are grown before the women serve prison sentences; by sentenc-
ing these young mothers to years of hard labor during their children's
youth, however, the government looked brutal (exactly as Pussy Riot
members have alleged).

Although the women of Pussy Riot did not usually emphasize
their own motherhood and the news media typically mentioned their
children only in passing laments, the fact of their maternity is still a
notable part of their story, not only as a significant part of their experience as individual women but also, and perhaps more importantly,
making their public image even more striking. By harshly punishing
two mothers with young children, the Russian government proved
the point of its critics: It cannot tolerate dissenting voices, even to
the point of squashing opposition with impunity. In the same way
that the name Pussy Riot evokes a range of meanings related not
only to female genitalia but also to revolt, chaos, and uprisings, the

306 "Crackdown in Russia," *60 Minutes* (CBS, March 24, 2013).

women of Pussy Riot *as mothers* suggest alternate roles of mother-hood. Moreover, like Perpetua and Felicitas, they seem to put aside maternity to participate in a public spectacle that is, at least in part, a protest of the current social order. Connections among these fig-ures illustrate the ways in which maternity is sometimes presented as conflicting with larger communal concerns and the ways in which women are sometimes condemned for their willingness to do things other than mother their biological children.

Perpetua, Felicitas, and Maternal Martyrdom

Like the narratives about Mary, the maternal figures in Revelation, and the Maccabean mother, this narrative begins *in media res*; that is, we encounter Perpetua, Felicitas, and their co-martyrs as characters only after their arrest (2.1).[307] Perpetua's diary itself begins, "While we were still under surveillance" (3.1) and proceeds from there. We do not hear about how the catechumens were discovered or arrested, whether they had any volition in the matter, or any of the details prior to their arrest. The arrest is just a fact on which the rest of the narrative rests. Commentators often focus on the element of choice that the catechumens seem to have in the trial scenes: because the judge and Perpetua's father encourage them to recant, it seems they could *choose* not to be executed. Perpetua's understanding, however, is diametrically opposed to theirs: she insists that, in the same way that a pitcher cannot be called anything else, she cannot "call [her-self] anything other than what [she is]: a Christian" (3.2). Burrus says,

> If the identity of the pitcher is secure, this is because it is "seen" ("do you see?" "I see"), and indeed one can easily imagine that it might be "called" by more than one name: Perpetua herself, after all, refers to it as both "vessel (*vas*)" and "little pitcher (*urceolum*)." In subtle contrast, the name of a Christian is fixed (she cannot and *will* not be called

---

[307] Bremmer, "Felicitas"; and Mieke Bal, "Perpetual Contest," in Bremmer and Formisano, *Perpetua's Passions*, 134–49.

anything else!), whereas its significance remains open to
interpretation: it remains to be seen.[308]

Perpetua's conception of her identity and her fate is fixed; she argues
that calling herself something else would not change her essence,
even as Burrus shows that this essence is also being constructed in
the text. Although many commentators tend to agree with her father
that Perpetua has options, Perpetua does not see a way to choose any
other course, and in fact, her interpretations of her visions tend to
emphasize the ways in which her fate is already sealed: "We realized
that we would have to suffer and that from now on we would no
longer have any hope in this life" (4.10) and "I realized that it was
not with wild animals that I would fight but with the devil" (10.14).

The competing allegiances presented in the *Passion of Perpetua
and Felicitas* are presented as diametrically opposed: biological family versus the adopted Christian family, civic responsibility versus
commitment to the community of catechumens, respect for the
paterfamilias versus fidelity to the martyr's true identity (as seen in
Perpetua's statement "I can't call myself anything other than what
I am: a Christian" [3.2]). Notions of family responsibility and family ties were in flux and were contested in the early centuries of the
Common Era; the politicization and promotion of certain family values as civic duties lurk behind these texts about Christian mothers
choosing martyrs' deaths over continued life with their young children. Emerging Christian identities seem to have promoted an openness to civic and familial discord in a way that other identities did
not; as discussed above, Bradley, van Henten, and others have compared Perpetua and Felicitas to the Maccabean mother to show the
ways in which certain Christian teachings encouraged rupture and
disconnection from one's family. This approach is indicative of certain common assumptions about these texts: Whereas the Maccabean
family members remain in solidarity and die as examples of familial,
civic, and religious harmony, Perpetua (and Felicitas, though only her
child is discussed) breaks ties with her biological family in order to

---

[308] Burrus, *Saving Shame*, 28.

die with her Christian family.[309] Bradley's assessment of the crowd's reaction to the Christian criminals indicates this overall assessment of the early Christians, whom he sees destroying the traditional family: "They [the spectators] saw Christians placing the interests of the individual far above the interests of the family, championing as a result an ethic completely at variance with traditional family values."[310]

We could read these competing alliances differently, however. First, interpreters sometimes have an exclusively biological definition of family, rather than seeing that family ties are also constructed through marriage and adoption, in addition to recognizing the broader scope of an ancient household[311]; this concept of family is treated as transcultural and transhistorical, as if "family" is always an essentialized, recognizable, and stable entity. Second, scholars often rely on a clear-cut notion of choice—related to the idea of family as ones you do not choose—as if Perpetua and Felicitas had every option open and simply chose a path they liked.[312] In some ways, this parallels the tendency in some media sources to fault the women of Pussy Riot for not considering the needs of their children when they protested in the cathedral. The Maccabean mother, in contrast, is usually seen as someone making necessary sacrifices rather than selfishly choosing something that hurts her children, yet there is much overlap between these texts, and Perpetua's character may even be modeled on the Maccabean mother.[313] It is also the case that their choices as *individuals* are often highlighted, rather than their self-alignment with an alternative community, one that they describe in familial terms. Although scholars may fault Perpetua and Felicitas for not champi-

---

[309] Compare with Van Henten, "*Passio Perpetuae*," 132–33.

[310] Bradley, "Sacrificing the Family," 173.

[311] See, for example, Beryl Rawson, ed., *The Family in Ancient Rome: New Perspectives* (Ithaca, NY: Cornell University Press, 1986); David Balch and Carolyn Osiek, eds., *Early Christian Families in Context: An Interdisciplinary Dialogue* (Grand Rapids, MI: Eerdmans, 2003); and Beryl Rawson, "'The Roman Family' in Recent Research: State of the Question," *Biblical Interpretation* 11, no. 2 (2003): 119–38.

[312] See, for example, Bremmer, "Felicitas," 51.

[313] Candida Moss, "Blood Ties: Martyrdom, Motherhood, and Family in the *Passion of Perpetua and Felicity*," in *Women and Gender in Ancient Religions: Interdisciplinary Approaches*, ed. Stephen P. Ahearne-Kroll, Paul A. Holloway, and James A. Kelhoffer (Tübingen: Mohr Siebeck, 2010), 192–93.

oning family values, the women rather champion family values different than those of the biological family and household.

The modern connection between family values (ostensibly a private matter) and the public sphere is by no means a newly forged alliance; Augustus famously used images of the imperial family to promote civic unity and particular forms of family structures as normative. The Ara Pacis Augustae includes idealized images of motherhood, childhood, and family life in a way that connects fertility with *pietas* and peace.[314] The so-called Augustan marriage legislation extended tangible benefits to certain kinds of kinship relations: The laws encouraged bearing a number of children and remaining married while they imposed penalties on celibacy and childlessness.[315]

Candida Moss focuses on the rejection of one's biological family as "a rather common feature of early Christian literature," one that is amplified in the portrayal of the female martyr.[316] Moss sees the ancient texts using this trope not to promote a "rejection of the idea of family, so much as they promote its reconfiguration."[317] She shows that the gender of the martyr strongly influences how interpreters respond to the texts:

> The scandal of Perpetua's rejection of her child, like the perceived callousness of the mother of the Maccabees, is a particularly gendered affair. Conversations about whether or not Socrates loves his children do not take place in scholarly analyses of his trial and death. His philosophical, not his parenting, skills are the issue. His abandonment of his biological and pedagogical children is hardly important. The mother of the Maccabees and the figure of Mary offer strong literary precedents for a mother preferring death (albeit that of her children) to a sustained earthly relationship with her child. Given the impact and status of these

---

[314] Zanker, *Power of Images in the Age of Augustus*, 172–79; Dixon, *Roman Mother*, 72–77.

[315] Rawson, "Roman Family," in *Family in Ancient Rome*, 9–10; Peskowitz, "'Family/ies' in Antiquity," 17.

[316] Moss, "Blood Ties," 189.

[317] Ibid., 190.

exempla in the early church, it is interesting that Perpetua's
behavior is viewed as extraordinary.[318] Perpetua's own salvation is at stake, yet her treament of her child continues
to be dissected and measured against modern standards of
motherhood.[319]

In the same way that modern debates inevitably configure work-fam-
ily balance as a "woman's issue," Perpetua and Felicitas's willingness
to leave their infants in order to be martyrs is that much more notable to modern interpreters precisely because Perpetua and Felicitas
are mothers. The oppressive and impossible "modern standards of
motherhood" that contemporary conversations invoke about stay-at-
home mothers versus working mothers, childcare arrangements, and
work-life balance are likewise part of the subtext in interpretations
of *The Passion of Perpetua and Felicitas*. Much of the psychoanalyzing
on the part of interpreters parallels the judgments of modern working mothers: "Mommy wars" can be waged in the interpretations of
ancient texts, too.[320]

   As with the women of Pussy Riot and other maternal activists
in general, Perpetua's maternity is connected to a broader horizon of
concern: In this text, she expresses concern and anxiety for her baby,
her family, her co-martyrs, and her dead brother. Especially in her
visions, there are themes of care and maternity, especially symbolized
in milk and other forms of feeding: In the shepherd dream, the shepherd gave Perpetua a mouthful of cheese, and, like a child who falls
asleep at the breast, she woke up "still chewing on something sweet"
(4.9) "as the densely intertextual dream metamorphizes the figure

---

[318] Here, Moss references a number of other scholars who express surprise and/or
horror at Perpetua's actions, among them Lefkowitz, "Motivations for St. Perpetua's
Martyrdom"; W. H. C. Frend, "Blandina and Perpetua: Two Early Christian Heroines,"
in *Women in Early Christianity*, ed. David M. Scholer (New York: Garland, 1993),
87–97; and Gillian Cloke, "*Mater* or Martyr: Christianity and the Alienation of
Women within the Family in the Later Roman Empire," *Theology and Sexuality* 3, no.
5 (September 1996): 37–57.
[319] Moss, "Blood Ties," 196.
[320] Ibid., 195. Moss and I are not referring to interpretations of this text that use a
psychoanalytic approach or perspective but rather to the approaches to this text that
psychoanalyze Perpetua as a character, as if she were stretched out on Freud's couch.

of a breast-feeding mother into that of a venerable shepherd, and Perpetua is identified not as the feeder but as the one fed."[321] Part of the drama of the initial chapters was related to how Perpetua's infant son will survive without her nursing: She was relieved when she could nurse him in prison, and finally relieved when he no longer needed to be nursed. Perpetua's prayers result in her dead brother's "release from his toils" (8.4), symbolized by his newfound ability to drink refreshing water and play "in the water the way little children do, gleefully" (8.4). The imagery of milk, drinking, childhood, sleep, and refreshment evokes a semantic field related to motherhood (and cf. her concerns about her son's physical need for her and his weaning in chapter 6, which precedes her visions about Dinocrates) and devoted care for another dependent body. Although Perpetua is sometimes seen as callous toward her son (and father, for that matter), the text emphasizes her anxiety for her son's needs and connects her mother-hood to other spheres of care.

Perpetua is sometimes faulted, then, for neglecting her baby and her father (her "real" family) and instead prioritizing her commit-ments and ties to her "artificial Christian family."[322] Queer theorists have helpfully pointed to the ways in which social marginalization can result in new familial commitments and alternative, queer, fam-ily structures; by equating blood relatives with nature and "reality," interpreters of the *Passion* do not always acknowledge that there are varied expressions of family, some entirely unrelated to biology.[323] Moreover, alternative conceptions of family and maternity may allow for broader expanded notions of ethics, care, and need. Perkins argues that the text's emphasis on maternity, especially the vulnerable body as a real universal, could have assuaged violence;[324] in the same way, an expanded vision of what family "is," to whom mothers extend their care, and who can make ethical demands on another, could also

---

[321] Burrus, *Saving Shame*, 29.
[322] Bradley, "Sacrificing the Family," 160.
[323] See, for example Kath Weston, *Families We Choose: Lesbians, Gays, Kinship*, Revised (New York: Columbia University Press, 1997); and Julie M. Thompson, *Mommy Queerest: Contemporary Rhetorics of Lesbian Maternal Identity* (Amherst: University of Massachusetts Press, 2002).
[324] Perkins, "Rhetoric of the Maternal Body," 314.

provide helpful openings toward a world in which people extend care to the Other, to strangers, to everyone.[325]

The transformation of Perpetua from mother, daughter, and matron to a veritable gladiator is a striking feature of the text and queers many readerly expectations about martyrs and their families.[326] Jennifer Koosed and Robert Paul Seesengood have shown that motherhood itself is queered in texts about mother-martyrs; by highlighting the ways in which biological motherhood involves loss of control, transformations of identity, the gift of life to another body, and violence done to the mother's body, Koosed and Seesengood suggest that the gender of a mother is unstable. This suggestion helps make sense of what most interpreters see as Perpetua's transformation; rather than seeing a stark contrast between Perpetua before and after her gender-bending dream, the interpretation of Koosed and Seesengood shows that Perpetua's gender has been unstable all along.[327] The same could be said of Felicitas, especially because she is a slave and, because of her lower status, would have been seen as less properly feminine than was Perpetua.[328] The use of maternal figures in a narrative that is, in part, about gender and pain indicates the ways in which maternity itself is an unstable, fluid gender categorization; moreover, this narrative betrays some of the anxieties about changing gender norms in the early centuries of the Common Era. The text uses mothers to reflect particularly on productive pain (even pain that is sought out, as Felicitas prays for labor to come so she might join her co-martyrs in the arena), as a notable parallel to martyrdom itself.

---

[325] Lisa Guenther, *The Gift of the Other: Levinas and the Politics of Reproduction* (Albany: State University of New York Press, 2006). Anna Rebecca Solevåg makes a similar point about the meaning of motherhood in the *Passion*; see her *Birthing Salvation: Gender and Class in Early Christian Childbearing Discourse* (Boston: Brill, 2013), 242.

[326] Koosed and Seesengood, "Queer Mothers."

[327] This pushes further than Cobb's interpretation, which suggests that the gender transformation is foreshadowed earlier in the text (see Cobb's *Dying to Be Men*, 97–105).

[328] Glancy, *Slavery in Early Christianity*, 16–21. See also Hartmut Böhme, who argues that Felicitas also undergoes a gender transformation: "Just as the *obstetrix* has no masculine form, the *retiarius* has no feminine form: in the transformation from one to the other, Felicitas undergoes a gender metamorphosis" ("The Conquest of the Real by the Imaginary: On the *Passio Perpetuae*," in Bremmer and Formisano, *Perpetua's Passions*, 227).

Maternity and martyrdom are thus closely linked: Martyr-mothers seek pain that is (re)productive and results in different, transformed bodies that are produced through brokenness and violence.

Conceptions of motherhood that include care, not only for proximate others (for example, one's own children) but also for distant others, might be a more productive way to consider the maternity of Perpetua and Felicitas. Certain notions of motherhood imply that mothers are naturally more nurturing and caring than non-mothers (male or female); feminists have rightly critiqued this essentializing of biological motherhood in at least two ways. First, the archetypal self-sacrificing mother often cares for others at her own expense (which is harmful both to her own self and to her children, whom she often seems to guilt into a certain kind of dependent relationship because of "all that she has done or given up" on their behalf). Additionally, connecting maternity automatically with care does not allow for that care to be a deliberate ethical choice that a mother makes; that is, care becomes something a mother must do—indeed, something she can't *not* do—instead of an intentional act of extending concern to another, an ethical stance that considers another's needs and wants.

Shannon Dunn, in her comparative reading of Perpetua and Wafa Idris (a Palestinian suicide bomber), attends to issues of gender norms and their regulation by martyrologists who remember these two female figures.[329] She notes, "Many contemporary scholars [for example, Perkins] read Perpetua's decision to leave her role in patriarchal Roman society as a paradigmatic theme in early Christian martyr literature: it constitutes an act of subversion against the oppressive powers of Rome."[330] Dunn instead sees Perpetua trading motherhood of an infant "for another form of parenthood (martyr of a community)"[331]; as Lieu has argued, the civic title "father" or "mother" functions in a particular way in early Christian and Jewish contexts, setting

---

[329] Shannon Dunn, "The Female Martyr and the Politics of Death." In his "Felicitas," Bremmer also compares Perpetua and Felicitas to modern suicide bombers.
[330] Dunn, "Female Martyr," 207, citing Perkins, *Suffering Self*.
[331] Ibid.

apart certain figures as models and leaders in their communities.[332] In their maternity, then, we can read Perpetua and Felicitas as venerated leaders who mother a community instead of mothering "only" their young children.

Maternal activists strategically capitalize on notions of maternal care as extending beyond one's own family to other people's children (and potentially to *all* others—nonhuman life included). Instead of faulting Perpetua and Felicitas for neglecting their biological children, interpreters might emphasize that the women ensure that their children will be raised by others—and that these mothers *also* care about others who are not biologically related to them. The women of Pussy Riot, moreover, discuss their visions for the future in ways that do not explicitly reference their motherhood; they believe that "openness and public speech and a hunger for the truth make us all a little bit freeer [*sic*]. We will see this yet."[333] Likewise, Perpetua and Felicitas face their chosen fate in hope with other members of their community, so instead of seeing their willingness to embrace death in the arena as selfish desire for self-fulfillment, interpreters could instead focus on the importance of the community in the text while also acknowledging that a martyrdom text itself can be read as deliberate defiance against continuing to live in a violent world.

As noted above, modern scholarship on Perpetua and Felicitas often occludes their status difference by highlighting their common role and experience as mothers, though John Marshall's observation that Perpetua does not even mention Felicitas in the diary portion of the *Passion* is a helpful corrective to this tendency. Anna Rebecca Solevåg likewise focuses on some of the differences between Perpetua and Felicitas, especially related to their status:

> Felicitas can be portrayed as someone struggling alone in labor, because of her low social status. Similarly, she is portrayed with breasts dripping when she enters the arena. Her

---

[332] Lieu, *Image and Reality*, 85. See chap. 3 of this book for a more extensive discussion of Lieu's insights.

[333] Translation of Maria Alyokhina's closing statement from Gessen, *Words Will Break Cement*, 216.

suffering and painful state is not negotiated [by the author, as Perpetua's is]. Motherhood includes extreme suffering, just as martyrdom does, and the body of the female slave is evidently a useful "site" to extrapolate this suffering. This is very different from the way in which the figure of Perpetua is explained and "rescued" from the dishonorable things that happen to her at every stage.[334]

Solevåg's discussion highlights the ways in which ancient mothers faced different expectations and pressures; in the same ways that upper-class white mothers in the United States face starkly different realities and social expectations than their lower-class nonwhite counterparts, Perpetua and Felicitas are portrayed as inhabiting different social worlds.[335] Shaw connects Perpetua's status, in particular, to memorializing these women when he writes,

> Something more than the problematic factor of gender was involved in the making of Perpetua's story. It is difficult to escape the conclusion that the important additional element that contributed forcefully to her memory was that of class. The public execution of a young lady of elevated social status in the amphitheatre at Carthage provoked the multiple responses in narratives, sermons, tracts and other kinds of mimicry by which her death was remembered. In this social setting, therefore, the fact of gender was strongly, if not decisively, modulated by that of class.[336]

Leaning on modern ideas about the shared common experiences of mothers occludes the ways in which status affects all aspects of a person's life, including experiences of family life. Moreover, ancient

---

[334] Anna Rebecca Solevåg, "Perpetua and Felicitas: Reinterpreting Empire, Family and Gender," in *Identity Formation in the New Testament*, ed. Bengt Holmberg and Mikael Winninge (Tübingen: Mohr Siebeck, 2008), 280. Solevåg expands this argument in her book, *Birthing Salvation*.

[335] See, for example, Ladd-Taylor and Umansky, *"Bad" Mothers*; and Hanigsberg and Ruddick, *Mother Troubles*.

[336] Shaw, "Passion of Perpetua," 325, quotation from his 2003 postscript.

lower-class women were sometimes portrayed as not suffering as much as their higher-status counterparts during pregnancy and child-birth, so describing the solidarity between Perpetua and Felicitas as based in their mothering is even more problematic.[337] Felicitas is described primarily related to her maternity; in this way, she is both like and unlike Perpetua, whose motherhood is one part of her iden-tity but not the only (or even primary?) part. Felicitas is a much flatter character, as she is mentioned only in the narrative frame of the text; she is not mentioned at all in Perpetua's or Saturus's prison diaries (which together comprise about half of the text's twenty-one chap-ters). Felicitas is named among the arrested catechumens in 2.1, and chapter 15 focuses exclusively on her labor; then, her experiences in the arena are narrated in 18.3–4 and 20.1–7, though her actual death is not mentioned. Fecund pain thus constitutes a major part of Felicitas's character. At the beginning of chapter 15, she is eight months pregnant and anticipating labor—more than anticipating, she is "very distressed that her martyrdom would be postponed because of her pregnancy, for it is against the law for women with child to be executed" (15.2). Like many pregnant women, Felicitas longs for labor and the end of pregnancy—but for unusual reasons: She wants to give a child life and then to embrace death in the arena. Her desire for labor is thus situated at a crossroads between death and life, much in the same way that martyrdom is framed as a death that brings life (that is, then, the reverse of what Felicitas prays for: a new life that will lead to her death). Martyrdom is even described as a kind of baptism, as Felicitas walks into the arena, "going from one blood bath to another, from the midwife to the gladiator, ready to wash after childbirth in a second baptism" (18.3).[338] Her longing for labor, then, somewhat ironically hints at the fragility of life as it is so closely wedded to death. Certain events, such as childbirth and martyrdom, throw into sharp relief the ways in which life and death are intertwined.

---

[337] Rousselle, *Porneia*, 43.
[338] Saturus also has a "second baptism" in 21.2. Solevåg also notes the framing of martyrdom as a second baptism(see her "Perpetua and Felicitas," 282).

A prison guard taunts Felicitas about her suffering in labor: "If this is how you suffer now, what will you do when you are thrown to the beasts, which you scorned when you refused to sacrifice?" (15.5). Felicitas answers, "What I am suffering now, I suffer by myself. But then [in the arena] another will be inside me who will suffer for me, just as I shall be suffering for him" (15.6–7). Her reply is sometimes interpreted as evidence of Montanism in this text: She emphasizes her "rigorous acceptance of martyrdom" and implies that shared suffering will be more manageable than what she is currently suffering alone.[339] Although her reply is usually interpreted pneumatologically (that is, that the Spirit will suffer for her; see also 16.1, where the Spirit permits and wills the spectacle and writing of this narrative), we could also read it as a Mariological reference: She suffers alone while birthing a child, whereas in the arena she will, like Mary, bear Jesus (or God, as a *Theotokos*) and they will suffer together. Her suffering is bearable because it is shared with others (and a divine Other), constructing a communal understanding of motherhood.

Felicitas's suffering, birthing body is a kind of metonymy for the arena: The longed-for pain produces a new (kind of) life and transformed bodies, even as it is also wedded to an expanded horizon of care. Pain, care, and transformative bodily changes are thus complexly linked. In chapter 15, focused on the delivery of her daughter, the comrades demonstrate concern for each other: Felicitas does not want to "shed her holy, innocent blood" with "common criminals," so her companions pray for her to deliver her baby early because "they were afraid that they would have to leave behind so fine a companion to travel alone on the same road to hope" (15.3). When the daughter is born, one of the sisters agrees to raise Felicitas's daughter after Felicitas dies.[340]

---

[339] Rex D. Butler, *The New Prophecy and "New Visions": Evidence of Montanism in* The Passion of Perpetua and Felicitas (Washington, DC: Catholic University of America Press, 2006), 85; Cecil M. Robeck, *Prophecy in Carthage: Perpetua, Tertullian, and Cyprian* (Cleveland, OH: Pilgrim, 1992), 287n28.

[340] Although the Latin reads simply *quam sibi quaedam soror in filiam educavit*, most interpreters assume this use of "sister" is metaphorical, pointing to a member of the Christian community who raises Felicitas's daughter as her own. See the discussion in Moss, "Blood Ties," 203n46, and Bremmer, "Felicitas," 45.

Mothering a Community

Maternal figures who embrace martyrdom invoke certain notions of maternity as care and as painful transformation; in this way, they also seem to gesture to the body of Jesus: a body broken "for you," a body transformed by suffering and redemptive in pain. The new bodies produced in motherhood, martyrdom, and the crucifixion hold death and life together: pain, brokenness, and death, but also the possibilities and promises of transformation and life. Thus, the figure of a mother is particularly productive when wrestling with these broader theo-ethical ideas.

Perkins's argument about the possibility for narratives like *The Passion of Perpetua and Felicitas* to assuage violence through the universality of the vulnerable body is persuasive in many ways; indeed, maternal activists utilize similar notions about the universality and essentialized nature of maternal care for other, vulnerable bodies, yet Perkins does not account for the possible harmful effects of this presentation. By referencing the broken, bleeding, leaking maternal body, the martyrologist does not disrupt but rather reinforces the connections among women's bodies and weakness, disgust, uncleanness, and animals. As with 4 Maccabees, some narrators mobilize maternal bodies rhetorically (even propagandistically) to argue theophilosophical points without taking care to assess the results for real mothers and other embodied persons.

The arguments I have presented here have some problematic implications, especially related to the idealization of Christian martyrs. By drawing connections between the narrative about Perpetua and Felicitas and the social dissent of the (maternal) activists of Pussy Riot, I risk presenting early Christian martyrdom as a purely admirable discourse and these figures as ideals, much in the same way that church tradition has admired martyrs for their courage and total devotion to God. The portrayal of martyrs as exclusively heroic has had detrimental effects on oppressed groups who have been told that sacrifice and submission are paths to eternal salvation—at the expense of their earthly well-being. Even more, these arguments risk portraying Perpetua and Felicitas's defiant actions as worthy of imitation, without acknowledging the losses, costs, and pitfalls of following in their footsteps.

Considering these figures alongside the women of Pussy Riot, however, may help interpreters see the ways in which Perpetua and Felicitas embody certain ideals (brave speech, truth-telling,[341] care for others in a community), while also seeing the various possible results of their actions. The women of Pussy Riot remain politically and socially active as of this writing, so the rest of their story remains to be written; although the end of Perpetua and Felicitas's story has been written, a variety of results and implications of the narrative exist, depending on the context of the interpreter. This open-endedness is welcome, as it may enable discussion and hope for a better future; in Alyokhina's words, "I believe that openness and public speech and a hunger for the truth make us all a little bit freer. We will see this yet."[342]

---

[341] Castelli, *Martyrdom and Memory*, 203.
[342] Quoted in Gessen, *Words Will Break Cement*, 216.

Conclusion: The Functions of Maternal Sacrifice

T hus far, I have explored thematic links among the narratives in each chapter (for example, violence, agency, loss, family, and nation) and have only hinted at some of the ways in which authors of later historical texts explicitly connect these figures. These connections are forged as early as the text of *The Passion of Perpetua and Felicitas* itself: Perpetua's fourth vision may be invoking Genesis 3:15 and/or Revelation 12,[343] both texts that are connected to Mary at later points in Christian theology.[344] By the mid-third century, at least two martyrdom texts linking Mary, the mother of the Maccabees, and Perpetua and Felicitas promote separation from one's natal family as part of true faithfulness to the Christian family. These mothers, who are presented as admirable and worthy of emulation, encourage their children to embrace death as a consequence of confessing the name "Christian" (*Martyrdom of Montanus and Lucius* 12.3; *Martyrdom of Marian and James* 7.6). In the *Martyrdom of Montanus and Lucius*, the mother of Flavian is praised as a "true daughter of Abraham" and "a mother of the race of the Maccabees" (16.3–6). In the *Martyrdom of Marian and James*, Marian's mother is described in even more adulatory terms, with the author noting that

> Marian's mother, now sure of her son once his passion was finished, rejoiced like the mother of the Maccabees, congratulating not only Marian but also herself that she had borne such a son. In the body of her son she embraced

---

[343] Musurillo, *Acts of the Christian Martyrs*, xxvi.
[344] Gail Paterson Corrington, *Her Image of Salvation: Female Saviors and Formative Christianity* (Louisville, KY: Westminster John Knox, 1992), 73; Glancy, *Corporal Knowledge*, 93–95.

the glory of her own womb; again and again with religious
devotion she pressed her lips to the wounds of his neck. Ah
mother, rightly called Mary, blessed are you in your son as
well as in your name! Surely no one could believe that in a
woman who was so honored by the offspring of her womb
the blessed fortune of so great a name would ever go astray!
(13.1–3)

Even through the mother's name ("rightly called Mary"), the author
of this martyrology deliberately links this mother to Mary and the
Maccabean mother, including emphasizing certainly bodily aspects
of motherhood and martyrdom: The mother embraces "the glory of
her own womb" (her son) and kisses "the wounds of his neck." Galit
Hasan-Rokem has shown the ways in which the fifth-century text
Lamentations Rabbah (considered in chapter 3) similarly links themes
from Perpetua's story to a narrative about a mother with seven sons,
here named Miriam/Mary. The complex narrative traditions connected to Mary, the female figures of Revelation, the Maccabean
mother, and Perpetua and Felicitas are related to ideals of self-control, resoluteness, enduring pain, and agency.

Mary, especially, continues to be evoked in more contemporary
moments. In the same ways in which the *madres* of Argentina explicitly connected their public protests to Mary's presence at the cross, the
members of COMADRES similarly frame their actions with reference
to Mary. Their founding statement describes Mary as devoted to her
son, as she "accompanied her son from birth to death and was present
at his resurrection. She did not ask what she was going to suffer along
the way, nor did she stop to think of the dangers."[345] The women of
Pussy Riot also invoked Mary and Marian devotion in their song criti-
cizing the Russian government's hegemony: Their "Punk Prayer" asks
Mary to put Putin in prison while also imploring her, "Virgin Mary,
Mother of God, become a feminist." These groups reframe traditional
notions of Mary (as a suffering mother, as one to whom prayers are
directed) in order to critique violent power structures and to demand

---

[345] Wright, *El Salvador*, 44.

justice for those who are hurt by the government. Why are mothers so particularly useful for these themes?

This exploration of discourses of self-sacrifice and martyrdom as they intersect with representations of mothers and their children in these texts disrupts the apparently natural connections between motherhood and sacrifice while also acknowledging the ways in which the mother-child relationship is particularly useful for ancient authors exploring the theme of self-denial, especially in contexts of sociopolitical violence. This acknowledgment helps us recognize and interrogate the various ways that conceptions of modern motherhood intersect with self-sacrifice, in ways that are both harmful to mothers and children and that might promote their flourishing.

Ancient images of self-sacrificing mothers (in various modes of sacrifice) were produced in a broad historical moment characterized by the emergence and negotiations of Jewish and Christian identities. The larger Greco-Roman world did not connect maternity with self-sacrifice as deliberately as these Jewish/Christian traditions, which place a mother with her children in a particularly violent context. This connection is not made in elite Greco-Roman discourses because the elites were not the ones experiencing violent subjugation. For ancient Jews and Christians, the self-sacrificing *mother* was useful in the context of emerging, contested, and subjugated identity production because maternal figures evoke notions of life, inheritance, transformative pain, and nurture. Moreover, the *self-sacrificing* mother is a synecdoche of the violent birth of a new identity: painful, full of risk, (re)productive, and in some way, inexorable, given the context of these narratives. The diversity of images of self-sacrificing mothers from early Jewish and Christian texts demonstrates that maternal self-sacrifice was a flexible discourse in antiquity, as it is today; these ancient maternal figures all experienced loss relating to their mothering, but neither their contexts nor their responses were identical. These texts situate mothers in contested situations that required complex responses (the mothers were not in control and did not have the choice to "have it all"), so these figures negotiated a number of different values or needs: their children's lives; their own lives; and questions of agency, loss, family, nation, religious devotion, and appropriate responses to violence. Thus, the various images of maternal self-sacrifice are not static; communities and authors portray these maternal figures in a few ways, as they conceive of maternal self-sacrifice as self-denial or submission, as a political strategy that uplifts a community, or as self-determination.

In some way, the image of a (religious) self-sacrificing mother in these ancient texts met an important psychological need in the audiences; these figures embody the ideal of altruism as they put others' needs before their own. Encountering a maternal figure (already associated with birth, pain, nurture, and care) who then sacrifices herself offers catharsis and addresses a real need, perhaps enabling the audience to imagine doing the same for another. In a community experiencing the birth pangs of a new life, this need may be even more urgent. The self-sacrificing mother thus embodies certain tensions or ideals about which the community has anxiety. Throughout my discussion of these texts, I have explored how these anxieties are related to three things: continuity, suffering, and community cohesion.

First, a self-sacrificing mother helps a community deal with questions of time and continuity. A parental figure represents a pivot or hinge that connects generations and is therefore also located at a point between the past and the future; that is, a parent symbolizes both what has been (history) and what might be (opportunity). Thus, a text with any parental figure can enable a community to wrestle with the complex negotiations required when both looking to the past and anticipating the future, as any community must. The mother's body, especially, with its highly visible changes that enable growth and new life, evokes a range of themes related to time, the future, hope, and eager anticipation.

Second, by reflecting on maternal self-sacrifice, a community can also consider whether and how pain can be productive. The pain of childbirth itself produces a new life or, rather, produces two new identities from one (a singular woman becomes a mother and child).[346] Moreover, the self-sacrificing mother, as one who births in

---

[346] For a brief summary of philosophical work on the maternal body, see Rachel Muers, *Living for the Future: Theological Ethics for Coming Generations* (New York: T & T Clark, 2008), 132–36; see also Guenther, *Gift of the Other*.

pain and accepts additional losses shows the ways in which self-sac-rifice can have complex possibilities for social protest. Violent losses oftentimes produce new, emerging identities (in Tertullian's lan-guage, "the blood of martyrs is seed" [*Apologeticus* 50]); the self-sacri-ficing mother likewise exemplifies the possibility that pain and loss may be necessary, or at least worthwhile. The other possibility also exists: The pain and loss may represent a Pyrrhic victory, at best, or a truly pitiful defeat.[347] Recent scholarly work on martyrdom and noble death enables us to further complicate these options; rather than see-ing that self-sacrifice is either effective or ineffective, we can instead see that if the fact of violent suffering comes first, then the expla-nation is a subsequent step. Because we experience loss that seems meaningless, communities and individuals attempt to make sense of it; narratives about maternal self-sacrifice are thus part of this larger move toward meaning making amid suffering.

Finally, textual representations of maternal self-sacrifice allow communities to negotiate the tension between the individual self and the other, especially as changing social norms cause a commu-nity to wrestle with the role of the individual in the larger commu-nity. Individuals in community must navigate between the Scylla and Charybdis of freedom and security; individuals in community cannot have absolute liberty (that would be anarchy), nor can a community with free individuals have absolute security (that would be tyranny). Whose needs are prioritized and when? The different expressions of maternal self-sacrifice considered in this book illuminate the vari-ous ways in which individuals in community can prioritize their own needs and the needs of the larger group—sometimes through sub-mission and sometimes through self-assertion. The experiences of maternal activists show the ways in which some actions or choices can involve both submission and self-assertion, prioritizing the well-being of both individuals and the community (or communities) as a whole.

These figures are thus part of the process by which groups forge a path toward cohesion and identity formation; these texts idealize

---

[347] Castelli, *Martyrdom and Memory*, 67.

maternal figures that choose self-sacrifice. Ideals help a group understand itself as a group and provide members with an example that they may strive to emulate. This could be done in localized ways: The Lukan community can look to Mary as an ideal, ancient Christians in North Africa can look to Perpetua and Felicitas, the *ekklesiae* of Asia Minor can look to the maternal figures in Revelation, Diaspora Jews can look to the Maccabean mother. This could also be the case in a macro sense as well: Jews and Christians in Greco-Roman antiquity had these various images of maternal self-sacrifice that helped them negotiate their identity as emerging, complex (and, indeed, separating) communities within a larger, violent imperial context. Having manifold images provides multiple entry points for communities to see themselves in the narratives, seeing the different kinds of idealized figures and the various results of their actions.

These various maternal images provide fertile space for reflecting on what motherhood "is" (in an essentialized way)—but also what it could be, might be, should be, or should not be. Highlighting the multiplicity of images leads to new possibilities for thinking of motherhood as self-sacrifice or for rejecting the connection between motherhood and self-sacrifice as necessary, or for attempting to hold the two in tension. That is, these figures allow audiences both ancient and modern to recognize that motherhood can involve loss and self-denial (but need not be defined as such) and to acknowledge the productive possibilities for social critique inherent in the images.

Motherhood is still a politically useful category and is often connected to notions of pain, loss, sacrifice, and self-denial. When mothers are portrayed as naturally self-sacrificing, we can interrogate the causes that are being promoted and the reasons for those agendas. If mothers are describing themselves as martyrs, then we can ask why and who benefits. If political or religious causes depend on the sacrifices of mothers (and others), we can look to the broader social circumstances that seem to demand their suffering. Because maternity is often linked to sacrifice so naturally, interrupting this inherent association enables us to interrogate the larger cultural forces that label all mothers as martyrs.

Selected Bibliography

This bibliography includes significant works about women, gender, and family relationships in antiquity (including the biblical figures considered in this book); early Christian and Jewish martyrdom; and feminist analyses of contemporary motherhood and maternal activism.

Ahearne-Kroll, Stephen P., Paul A. Holloway, and James A. Kelhoffer, eds. *Women and Gender in Ancient Religions: Interdisciplinary Approaches*. Tübingen: Mohr Siebeck, 2010.

Alegria, Claribel. *They Won't Take Me Alive: Salvadorean Women in Struggle for National Liberation*. Translated by Amanda Hopkinson. London: Women's Press, 1983.

Althaus-Reid, Marcella. *Indecent Theology: Theological Perversions in Sex, Gender, and Politics*. New York: Routledge, 2000.

Anderson, Janice Capel. "Mary's Difference: Gender and Patriarchy in the Birth Narratives." *Journal of Religion* 67, no. 2 (April 1987): 183–202.

Aune, David E. *Revelation 1–5*. Word Biblical Commentary 52A. Dallas: Word Publishers, 1997.

———. *Revelation 6–16*. Word Biblical Commentary 52B. Nashville, TN: Thomas Nelson, 1998.

———. *Revelation 17–22*. Word Biblical Commentary 52C. Nashville, TN: Thomas Nelson, 1998.

Badinter, Elisabeth. *Mother Love: Myth and Reality*. New York: Macmillan, 1981.

Bal, Mieke. "Perpetual Contest." In *Perpetua's Passions: Multidisciplinary Approaches to the* Passio Perpetuae et Felicitatis, edited by Jan N. Bremmer and Marco Formisano, 134–49. New York: Oxford University Press, 2012.

Balch, David, and Carolyn Osiek, eds. *Early Christian Families in Context: An Interdisciplinary Dialogue.* Grand Rapids, MI: Eerdmans, 2003.

Becker, Adam H., and Annette Yoshiko Reed, eds. *The Ways that Never Parted: Jews and Christians in Late Antiquity and the Early Middle Ages.* Minneapolis, MN: Fortress, 2003.

Binford, Leigh. *The El Mozote Massacre: Anthropology and Human Rights.* Tucson: University of Arizona Press, 1996.

Boff, Clodovis. "Toward a Social Mariology." In *The Many Faces of Mary,* edited by Diego Irarrazaval, Susan Ross, and Marie-Theres Wacker, 43–56. Concilium 2008, No. 4. London: SCM Press, 2008.

Böhme, Hartmut. "The Conquest of the Real by the Imaginary: On the Passio Perpetuae." In *Perpetua's Passions: Multidisciplinary Approaches to the* Passio Perpetuae et Felicitatis, edited by Jan N. Bremmer and Marco Formisano, 220–43. New York: Oxford University Press, 2012.

Boss, Sarah Jane. *Mary.* New York: Continuum, 2004.

———, ed. *Mary: The Complete Resource.* London: Oxford University Press, 2007.

Bousquet, Jean-Pierre. *Las Locas de La Plaza de Mayo.* Buenos Aires: El Cid Editor, 1983.

Bouvard, Marguerite Guzman. *Revolutionizing Motherhood: The Mothers of the Plaza de Mayo.* Wilmington, DE: Scholarly Resources, 1994.

Bowersock, G. W. *Martyrdom and Rome.* Cambridge: Cambridge University Press, 1995.

Boyarin, Daniel. *Border Lines: The Partition of Judaeo-Christianity.* Philadelphia: University of Pennsylvania Press, 2004.

———. *Dying for God: Martyrdom and the Making of Christianity and Judaism.* Stanford, CA: Stanford University Press, 1999.

———. "Masada or Yavneh? Gender and the Arts of Jewish Resistance." In *Jews and Other Differences: The New Jewish Cultural Studies,* edited by Jonathan Boyarin and Daniel Boyarin, 306–29. Minneapolis: University of Minnesota Press, 1997.

Bradley, Keith R. *Discovering the Roman Family: Studies in Roman Social History.* New York: Oxford University Press, 1991.

———. "Sacrificing the Family: Christian Martyrs and Their Kin." *Ancient Narrative* 3 (2003): 150–81.

Bremmer, Jan N. "Felicitas: The Martyrdom of a Young African Woman." In *Perpetua's Passions: Multidisciplinary Approaches to the* Passio Perpetuae et Felicitatis, edited by Jan N. Bremmer and Marco Formisano, 35–53. New York: Oxford University Press, 2012.

Bremmer, Jan N., and Marco Formisano, eds. *Perpetua's Passions: Multidisciplinary Approaches to the* Passio Perpetuae et Felicitatis. New York: Oxford University Press, 2012.

Brown, Raymond E. *The Birth of the Messiah: A Commentary on the Infancy Narratives in the Gospels of Matthew and Luke.* Updated ed. New York: Doubleday, 1993.

Brown, Raymond E., Joseph A. Fitzmyer, Karl P. Donfried, and John Reumann, eds. *Mary in the New Testament: A Collaborative Assessment by Protestant and Roman Catholic Scholars.* Philadelphia: Fortress, 1978.

Buell, Denise Kimber. *Making Christians: Clement of Alexandria and the Rhetoric of Legitimacy.* Princeton, NJ: Princeton University Press, 1999.

———. *Why This New Race? Ethnic Reasoning in Early Christianity.* New York: Columbia University Press, 2005.

Burrus, Virginia. *Saving Shame: Martyrs, Saints, and Other Abject Subjects.* Philadelphia: University of Pennsylvania Press, 2008.

———. "Torture and Travail: Producing the Christian Martyr." In *A Feminist Companion to Patristic Literature*, edited by Amy-Jill Levine, 56–71. London: T & T Clark, 2008.

Butler, Rex D. *The New Prophecy and "New Visions": Evidence of Montanism in* The Passion of Perpetua and Felicitas. Washington, DC: Catholic University of America Press, 2006.

Carr, Anne, and Elisabeth Schüssler Fiorenza, eds. *Motherhood: Experience, Institution, Theology.* Edinburgh: T & T Clark, 1989.

Carr, Anne E., and Mary Stewart Van Leeuwen, eds. *Religion, Feminism, and the Family.* Louisville, KY: Westminster John Knox, 1996.

Castelli, Elizabeth A. *Martyrdom and Memory: Early Christian Culture Making.* New York: Columbia University Press, 2004.

Castelli, Elizabeth A., and Hal Taussig, eds. *Reimagining Christian Origins: A Colloquium Honoring Burton L. Mack.* Valley Forge, PA: Trinity Press International, 1996.

Cloke, Gillian. "*Mater* or Martyr: Christianity and the Alienation of Women within the Family in the Later Roman Empire." *Theology and Sexuality* 3, no. 5 (1996): 37–57.

Cobb, L. Stephanie. *Dying to Be Men: Gender and Language in Early Christian Martyr Texts*. New York: Columbia University Press, 2008.

Cohen, Shaye J. D. *The Beginnings of Jewishness: Boundaries, Varieties, Uncertainties*. Berkeley: University of California Press, 1999.

———, ed. *The Jewish Family in Antiquity*. Atlanta: Scholars, 1993.

Cooey, Paula M. "'Ordinary Mother' as Oxymoron: The Collusion of Theology, Theory, and Politics in the Undermining of Mothers." In *Mother Troubles: Rethinking Contemporary Maternal Dilemmas*, edited by Julia E. Hanigsberg and Sara Ruddick, 229–49. Boston: Beacon Press, 1999.

Cooper, Kate. *The Virgin and the Bride: Idealized Womanhood in Late Antiquity*. Cambridge, MA: Harvard University Press, 1996.

Copier, Laura. "Maternal Martyrdom: *Alien3* and the Power of the Female Martyr." In *Powers: Religion as a Social and Spiritual Force*, edited by Meerten B. ter Borg and Jan Willem van Henten, 275–91. New York: Oxford University Press, 2010.

Corrado Pope, Barbara. "Immaculate and Powerful: The Marian Revival in the Nineteenth Century." In *Immaculate and Powerful: The Female in Sacred Image and Social Reality*, 173–200. Boston: Beacon, 1985.

Corrington, Gail Paterson. *Her Image of Salvation: Female Saviors and Formative Christianity*. Louisville, KY: Westminster John Knox, 1992.

———. *See also* Streete, Gail Corrington *or* Streete, Gail P. C.

Crowder, Stephanie Buckhanon. *When Momma Speaks: The Bible and Motherhood from a Womanist Perspective*. Louisville, KY: Westminster John Knox, 2016.

D'Angelo, Mary Rose. "*Eusebeia*: Roman Imperial Family Values and the Sexual Politics of 4 *Maccabees* and the Pastorals." *Biblical Interpretation* 11, no. 2 (2003): 139–65.

Dean-Jones, Lesley. *Women's Bodies in Classical Greek Science*. New York: Oxford University Press, 1994.

Demand, Nancy. *Birth, Death, and Motherhood in Classical Greece*. Baltimore, MD: Johns Hopkins University Press, 1994.

DeSilva, David A. *4 Maccabees: Introduction and Commentary on the Greek Text in Codex Sinaiticus*. Septuagint Commentary Series. Leiden: Brill, 2006.

Dewey, Joanna. "Sacrifice No More." In *Distant Voices Drawing Near: Essays in Honor of Antoinette Clark Wire*, edited by Holly E. Hearon, 159–70. Collegeville, MN: Liturgical Press, 2004.

Dixon, Suzanne. *The Roman Family*. Baltimore, MD: Johns Hopkins University Press, 1992.

———. *The Roman Mother*. Norman: University of Oklahoma Press, 1988.

Doran, Robert. *2 Maccabees: A Critical Commentary*. Hermeneia. Minneapolis, MN: Augsburg Fortress, 2012.

———. "The Martyr: A Synoptic View of the Mother and Her Seven Sons." In *Ideal Figures in Ancient Judaism: Profiles and Paradigms*, edited by John J. Collins and George W. E. Nickelsburg, 189–221. Missoula, MT: Scholars, 1980.

Dunn, Shannon. "The Female Martyr and the Politics of Death: An Examination of the Martyr Discourses of Vibia Perpetua and Wafa Idris." *Journal of the American Academy of Religion* 78, no. 1 (March 2010): 202–25.

Evans, Suzanne. *Mothers of Heroes, Mothers of Martyrs: World War I and the Politics of Grief*. Montreal: McGill-Queen's University Press, 2007.

Foskett, Mary F. *A Virgin Conceived: Mary and Classical Representations of Virginity*. Bloomington: Indiana University Press, 2002.

Frend, W. H. C. "Blandina and Perpetua: Two Early Christian Heroines." In *Women in Early Christianity*, edited by David M. Scholer, 87–97. New York: Garland, 1993.

———. *Martyrdom and Persecution in the Early Church: A Study of a Conflict from the Maccabees to Donatus*. Oxford: Blackwell, 1965.

Frilingos, Christopher A. *Spectacles of Empire: Monsters, Martyrs, and the Book of Revelation*. Philadelphia: University of Pennsylvania Press, 2004.

Gaventa, Beverly Roberts. "'All Generations Will Call Me Blessed': Mary in Biblical and Ecumenical Perspective." In *A Feminist Companion to Mariology*, edited by Amy-Jill Levine and Maria Mayo Robbins, 121–29. Cleveland, Oh.: Pilgrim Press, 2005.

———. *Mary: Glimpses of the Mother of Jesus*. Columbia: University of South Carolina Press, 1995.

————, and Cynthia Rigby, eds. *Blessed One: Protestant Perspectives on Mary*. Louisville, KY: Westminster John Knox, 2002.

Gessen, Masha. *Words Will Break Cement: The Passion of Pussy Riot*. New York: Riverhead, 2014.

Gibson, Leigh, and Shelly Matthews, eds. *Violence in the New Testament*. New York: T & T Clark, 2005.

Glancy, Jennifer A. *Corporal Knowledge: Early Christian Bodies*. New York: Oxford University Press, 2010.

————. *Slavery in Early Christianity*. New York: Oxford University Press, 2002.

————, and Stephen D. Moore. "How Typical a Roman Prostitute Is Revelation's 'Great Whore'?" *Journal of Biblical Literature* 130, no. 3 (2011): 551–69.

Good, Deirdre J., ed. *Mariam, the Magdalen, and the Mother*. Bloomington: Indiana University Press, 2005.

Grenholm, Cristina. *Motherhood and Love: Beyond the Gendered Stereotypes of Theology*. Translated by Marie Tåqvist. Grand Rapids, MI: Eerdmans, 2011.

Guenther, Lisa. *The Gift of the Other: Levinas and the Politics of Reproduction*. Albany: State University of New York Press, 2006.

Haber, Susan. "Living and Dying for the Law: The Mother-Martyrs of 2 Maccabees." *Women in Judaism: A Multidisciplinary Journal* 4, no. 1 (Winter 2006).

Hallett, Judith P. "Introduction: Cornelia and Her Maternal Legacy." *Helios* 33, no. 2 (Fall 2006): 119–47.

Hanigsberg, Julia E., and Sara Ruddick, eds. *Mother Troubles: Rethinking Contemporary Maternal Dilemmas*. Boston: Beacon, 1999.

Henten, Jan Willem van. *The Maccabean Martyrs as Saviours of the Jewish People: A Study of 2 and 4 Maccabees*. Leiden: Brill, 1997.

————. "The *Passio Perpetuae* and Jewish Martyrdom: The Motif of Motherly Love." In *Perpetua's Passions: Multidisciplinary Approaches to the* Passio Perpetuae et Felicitatis, edited by Jan N. Bremmer and Marco Formisano, 118–33. New York: Oxford University Press, 2012.

Huber, Lynn R. *Like a Bride Adorned: Reading Metaphor in John's Apocalypse*. New York: T & T Clark International, 2007.

Ibáñez, Ana Cristina. "El Salvador: War and Untold Stories: Women Guerrillas." In *Victims, Perpetrators, or Actors? Gender, Armed*

Conflict, and Political Violence, edited by Caroline O. N. Moser and Fiona C. Clark, 117–30. New York: Zed, 2001.

Irarrazaval, Diego, Susan Ross, and Marie-Theres Wacker, eds. *The Many Faces of Mary*. Concilium 2008, No. 4. London: SCM, 2008.

Jacob, Sharon. *Reading Mary Alongside Indian Surrogate Mothers: Violent Love, Oppressive Liberation, and Infancy Narratives*. New York: Palgrave Macmillan, 2015.

Jetter, Alexis, Annelise Orleck, and Diana Taylor, eds. *The Politics of Motherhood: Activist Voices from Left to Right*. Hanover, NH: University Press of New England, 1997.

Johnson, Elizabeth A. *Dangerous Memories: A Mosaic of Mary in Scripture*. New York: Continuum, 2004.

———. *Truly Our Sister: A Theology of Mary in the Communion of Saints*. New York: Continuum, 2003.

Johnson-DeBaufre, Melanie. "Communities Resisting Fragmentation: Q and the Work of James C. Scott." In *Oral Performance, Popular Tradition, and Hidden Transcript in Q*, edited by Richard A. Horsley, 193–207. Semeia Studies 60. Atlanta: Society of Biblical Literature, 2006.

———. *Jesus among Her Children: Q, Eschatology, and the Construction of Christian Origins*. Cambridge, MA: Harvard University Press, 2005.

Joshel, Sandra R., and Sheila Murnaghan, eds. *Women and Slaves in Greco-Roman Culture: Differential Equations*. New York: Routledge, 1998.

Joslyn-Siemiatkoski, Daniel. *Christian Memories of the Maccabean Martyrs*. New York: Palgrave Macmillan, 2009.

Kawash, Samira. "New Directions in Motherhood Studies." *Signs* 36, no. 4 (June 2011): 969–1003.

Kearns, Cleo McNelly. *The Virgin Mary, Monotheism, and Sacrifice*. New York: Cambridge University Press, 2008.

Keller, Catherine. *Apocalypse Now and Then: A Feminist Guide to the End of the World*. Boston: Beacon, 1996.

Kessler, Gwynn. *Conceiving Israel: The Fetus in Rabbinic Narratives*. Philadelphia: University of Pennsylvania Press, 2009.

Kim, Jean K. *Woman and Nation: An Intercontextual Reading of the Gospel of John from a Postcolonial Feminist Perspective*. Boston: Brill, 2004.

King, Helen. *Hippocrates' Woman: Reading the Female Body in Ancient Greece*. New York: Routledge, 1998.

Kirk-Duggan, Cheryl A., and Tina Pippin, eds. *Mother Goose, Mother Jones, Mommie Dearest: Biblical Mothers and Their Children*. Atlanta, GA: Society of Biblical Literature, 2009.

Kraemer, Ross Shepard. *Unreliable Witnesses: Religion, Gender, and History in the Greco-Roman Mediterranean*. New York: Oxford University Press, 2011.

———. "When Is a Text about a Woman a Text about a Woman? The Cases of Aseneth and Perpetua." In *A Feminist Companion to Patristic Literature*, edited by Amy-Jill Levine and Maria Mayo Robbins, 156–72. London: T & T Clark, 2008.

———, and Mary Rose D'Angelo, eds. *Women and Christian Origins*. New York: Oxford University Press, 1999.

Ladd-Taylor, Molly, and Lauri Umansky, eds. *"Bad" Mothers: The Politics of Blame in Twentieth-Century America*. New York: New York University Press, 1998.

Lefkowitz, Mary R. "Motivations for St. Perpetua's Martyrdom." *Journal of the American Academy of Religion* 44, no. 3 (Summer 1976): 417–21.

Levine, Amy-Jill, ed. *"Women Like This": New Perspectives on Jewish Women in the Greco-Roman World*. Atlanta, GA: Scholars, 1991.

———, and Maria Mayo Robbins, eds. *A Feminist Companion to Mariology*. Cleveland, OH: Pilgrim, 2005.

Lieu, Judith. *Image and Reality: The Jews in the World of the Christians in the Second Century*. Edinburgh: T & T Clark, 1996.

———. *Neither Jew Nor Greek? Constructing Early Christianity*. New York: T & T Clark, 2002.

López, Rosa María Cid, ed. *Madres y Maternidades: Construcciones Culturales en la Civilización Clásica*. Oviedo: KRK Ediciones, 2009.

Lozano-Diaz, Nora O. "Ignored Virgin or Unaware Women: A Mexican-American Protestant Reflection on the Virgin of Guadalupe." In *Blessed One: Protestant Perspectives on Mary*, edited by Beverly Roberts Gaventa and Cynthia Rigby, 85–96. Louisville, Ky.: Westminster John Knox Press, 2002.

Maeckelberghe, Els. *Desperately Seeking Mary: A Feminist Appropriation of a Traditional Religious Symbol*. Kampen, The Netherlands: Pharos, 1991.

Malcolm, Lois. "What Mary Has to Say about God's Bare Goodness." In *Blessed One: Protestant Perspectives on Mary*, edited by Beverly Roberts Gaventa and Cynthia Rigby, 131–44. Louisville, Ky.: Westminster John Knox Press, 2002.

Martin, Dale B. "The Construction of the Ancient Family: Methodological Considerations." *Journal of Roman Studies* 86 (January 1996): 40–60.

Mason, Steve. "Jews, Judaeans, Judaizing, Judaism: Problems of Categorization in Ancient History." *Journal for the Study of Judaism* 38, no. 4 (2007): 457–512.

Matthews, Shelly. *Perfect Martyr: The Stoning of Stephen and the Construction of Christian Identity*. New York: Oxford University Press, 2010.

———. "Thinking of Thecla: Issues in Feminist Historiography." *Journal of Feminist Studies in Religion* 17, no. 2 (Fall 2001): 39–55.

Maunder, Chris. *Origins of the Cult of the Virgin Mary*. New York: Burns & Oates, 2008.

Mercedes, Anna. *Power For: Feminism and Christ's Self-Giving*. New York: T & T Clark, 2011.

Migliore, Daniel L. "Woman of Faith: Toward a Reformed Understanding of Mary." In *Blessed One: Protestant Perspectives on Mary*, edited by Beverly Roberts Gaventa and Cynthia Rigby, 117–30. Louisville, Ky.: Westminster John Knox Press, 2002.

Miller-McLemore, Bonnie. *Also a Mother: Work and Family as Theological Dilemma*. Nashville, TN: Abingdon, 1994.

———. "Ideals and Realities of Motherhood: A Theological Perspective." In *Mother Troubles: Rethinking Contemporary Maternal Dilemmas*, edited by Julia E. Hanigsberg and Sara Ruddick, 281–303. Boston: Beacon Press, 1999.

———. "'Pondering All These Things': Mary and Motherhood." In *Blessed One: Protestant Perspectives on Mary*, edited by Beverly Roberts Gaventa and Cynthia Rigby, 97–114. Louisville, Ky.: Westminster John Knox Press, 2002.

Moore, Stephen D. *Empire and Apocalypse: Postcolonialism and the New Testament*. Sheffield, England: Sheffield Phoenix, 2006.

———. *God's Beauty Parlor: And Other Queer Spaces in and around the Bible*. Stanford, CA: Stanford University Press, 2001.

————, and Janice Capel Anderson. "Taking It like a Man: Masculinity in 4 Maccabees." *Journal of Biblical Literature* 117, no. 2 (1998): 249–73.

Moss, Candida R. *Ancient Christian Martyrdom: Diverse Practices, Theologies, and Traditions.* New Haven, CT: Yale University Press, 2012.

Moxnes, Halvor, ed. *Constructing Early Christian Families: Family as Social Reality and Metaphor.* London: Routledge, 1997.

Musurillo, Herbert, trans. *The Acts of the Christian Martyrs.* Oxford: Clarendon Press, 1972.

Nathan, Geoffrey S. *The Family in Late Antiquity: The Rise of Christianity and the Endurance of Tradition.* New York: Routledge, 2000.

Nathanson, Janice. "Maternal Activism: How Feminist Is It?" In *Feminist Mothering,* edited by Andrea O'Reilly, 243–56. Albany: State University of New York Press, 2008.

Newsom, Carol A., Sharon H. Ringe, and Jacqueline E. Lapsley, eds. *Women's Bible Commentary.* Revised and updated 3rd ed. Louisville, KY: Westminster John Knox, 2012.

O'Reilly, Andrea, ed. *Feminist Mothering.* Albany: State University of New York Press, 2008.

————. *From Motherhood to Mothering: The Legacy of Adrienne Rich's Of Woman Born.* Albany: State University of New York Press, 2004.

————. *Maternal Theory: Essential Readings.* Toronto: Demeter, 2007.

————. *Twenty-First Century Motherhood: Experience, Identity, Policy, Agency.* New York: Columbia University Press, 2010.

Osiek, Carolyn. "*Pietas* in and out of the Frying Pan." *Biblical Interpretation* 11, no. 2 (2003): 166–72.

————, and David Balch. *Families in the New Testament World: Households and House Churches.* Louisville, KY: Westminster John Knox, 1997.

————, and Margaret Y. MacDonald. *A Woman's Place: House Churches in Earliest Christianity.* Minneapolis, MN: Fortress, 2006.

Pelikan, Jaroslav. *Mary through the Centuries: Her Place in the History of Culture.* New Haven, CT: Yale University Press, 1996.

Perkins, Judith. *Roman Imperial Identities in the Early Christian Era.* London: Routledge, 2009.

————. *The Suffering Self: Pain and Narrative Representation in the Early Christian Era.* New York: Routledge, 1995.

Petersen, Lauren Hackworth, and Patricia Salzman-Mitchell, eds. *Mothering and Motherhood in Ancient Greece and Rome*. Austin: University of Texas Press, 2012.

Phillips, Gary A. "The Killing Fields of Matthew's Gospel." In *A Shadow of Glory: Reading the New Testament after the Holocaust*, edited by Tod Linafelt, 232–47. New York: Routledge, 2002.

———. "More Than the Jews . . . His Blood Be upon All the Children: Biblical Violence, Genocide, and Responsible Reading." In *Confronting Genocide: Judaism, Christianity, Islam*, edited by Steven L. Jacobs, 77–93. Lanham, MD: Lexington, 2009.

Pippin, Tina. *Apocalyptic Bodies: The Biblical End of the World in Text and Image*. New York: Routledge, 1999.

———. *Death and Desire: The Rhetoric of Gender in the Apocalypse of John*. Louisville, KY: Westminster John Knox, 1992.

Poe, Danielle. *Maternal Activism: Mothers Confronting Injustice*. Albany: State University of New York Press, 2015.

Purvis, Sally B. "Mothers, Neighbors, and Strangers: Another Look at *Agape*." *Journal of Feminist Studies in Religion* 7, no. 1 (Spring 1991): 19–34.

Rawson, Beryl, ed. *The Family in Ancient Rome: New Perspectives*. Ithaca, NY: Cornell University Press, 1986.

———, ed. *Marriage, Divorce, and Children in Ancient Rome*. New York: Oxford University Press, 1991.

———. "'The Roman Family' in Recent Research: State of the Question." *Biblical Interpretation* 11, no. 2 (2003): 119–38.

Reeder, Caryn A. "Pity the Women and Children: Punishment by Siege in Josephus's *Jewish War*." *Journal for the Study of Judaism* 44, no. 2 (Spring 2013): 1–21.

Rhoads, David M. *From Every People and Nation: The Book of Revelation in Intercultural Perspective*. Minneapolis, MN: Fortress, 2005.

Rich, Adrienne. *Of Woman Born: Motherhood as Experience and Institution*. New York: Norton, 1976.

Rigby, Cynthia. "Mary and the Artistry of God." In *Blessed One: Protestant Perspectives on Mary*, edited by Beverly Roberts Gaventa and Cynthia Rigby, 145–58. Louisville, Ky.: Westminster John Knox Press, 2002.

Rossing, Barbara R. *The Choice between Two Cities: Whore, Bride, and Empire in the Apocalypse*. Harrisburg, PA: Trinity Press International, 1999.

Rousselle, Aline. *Porneia: On Desire and the Body in Antiquity*. New York: Blackwell, 1988.

Ruddick, Sara. *Maternal Thinking: Toward a Politics of Peace*. Boston: Beacon, 1989.

Ruether, Rosemary Radford. *Sexism and God-Talk: Toward a Feminist Theology*. Boston: Beacon, 1983.

Saiving, Valerie. "The Human Situation: A Feminine View." *Journal of Religion* 40, no. 2 (1960): 100–112.

Salisbury, Joyce E. *The Blood of Martyrs: Unintended Consequences of Ancient Violence*. New York: Routledge, 2004.

Satlow, Michael L. *Jewish Marriage in Antiquity*. Princeton, NJ: Princeton University Press, 2001.

Schaberg, Jane. *The Illegitimacy of Jesus: A Feminist Theological Interpretation of the Infancy Narratives*. Expanded twentieth anniversary ed. Sheffield, England: Sheffield Phoenix, 2006.

———. *The Resurrection of Mary Magdalene: Legends, Apocrypha, and the Christian Testament*. New York: Continuum, 2004.

Scheper-Hughes, Nancy. *Death without Weeping: The Violence of Everyday Life in Brazil*. Berkeley: University of California Press, 1992.

Schüssler Fiorenza, Elisabeth. *Jesus and the Politics of Interpretation*. New York: Continuum, 2000.

———. *Jesus: Miriam's Child, Sophia's Prophet: Critical Issues in Feminist Christology*. New York: Continuum, 1994.

———. *Rhetoric and Ethic: The Politics of Biblical Studies*. Minneapolis, MN: Fortress, 1999.

———, ed. *Searching the Scriptures: A Feminist Introduction and Commentary*. 2 vols. New York: Crossroad, 1993–1994.

———. *Wisdom Ways: Introducing Feminist Biblical Interpretation*. Maryknoll, NY: Orbis, 2001.

Schwartz, Daniel R. *2 Maccabees*. Berlin: Walter de Gruyter, 2008.

Schwartz, Seth. *Imperialism and Jewish Society, 200 BCE to 640 CE*. Princeton, NJ: Princeton University Press, 2001.

———. *Were the Jews a Mediterranean Society? Reciprocity and Solidarity in Ancient Judaism*. Princeton, NJ: Princeton University Press, 2010.

Shaw, Brent D. "Body/Power/Identity: Passions of the Martyrs." *Journal of Early Christian Studies* 4, no. 3 (Fall 1996): 269–312.

————. "The Passion of Perpetua." *Past and Present*, no. 139 (May 1993): 3–45.

————. "The Passion of Perpetua." In *Studies in Ancient Greek and Roman Society*, edited by Robin Osborne, 286–325. New York: Cambridge University Press, 2004.

Shepkaru, Shmuel. *Jewish Martyrs in the Pagan and Christian Worlds*. New York: Cambridge University Press, 2006.

Sissa, Giulia. *Greek Virginity*. Cambridge, MA: Harvard University Press, 1990.

Skaine, Rosemarie. *Female Suicide Bombers*. Jefferson, NC: McFarland, 2006.

Smith, Shanell T. *The Woman Babylon and the Marks of Empire: Reading Revelation with a Postcolonial Womanist Hermeneutics of Ambiveilence*. Minneapolis, MN: Fortress, 2014.

Solevåg, Anna Rebecca. *Birthing Salvation: Gender and Class in Early Christian Childbearing Discourse*. Boston: Brill, 2013.

————. "Perpetua and Felicitas: Reinterpreting Empire, Family, and Gender." In *Identity Formation in the New Testament*, edited by Bengt Holmberg and Mikael Winninge, 269–84. Tübingen: Mohr Siebeck, 2008.

Stitt, Jocelyn Fenton, and Pegeen Reichert Powell, eds. *Mothers Who Deliver: Feminist Interventions in Public and Interpersonal Discourse*. Albany: State University of New York Press, 2010.

Streete, Gail Corrington. *The Strange Woman: Power and Sex in the Bible*. Louisville, KY: Westminster John Knox, 1997.

————. *See also* Corrington, Gail Paterson, *or* Streete, Gail P. C.

Streete, Gail P. C. "Of Martyrs and Men: Perpetua, Thecla, and the Ambiguity of Female Heroism in Early Christianity." In *The Subjective Eye: Essays in Culture, Religion, and Gender in Honor of Margaret R. Miles*, edited by Richard Valantasis. Eugene, OR: Pickwick, 2006.

————. *Redeemed Bodies: Women Martyrs in Early Christianity*. Louisville, KY: Westminster John Knox, 2009.

————. *See also* Corrington, Gail Paterson, *or* Streete, Gail Corrington.

Taylor, Diana. *Disappearing Acts: Spectacles of Gender and Nationalism in Argentina's "Dirty War."* Durham, NC: Duke University Press, 1997.

Thompson, Julie M. *Mommy Queerest: Contemporary Rhetorics of Lesbian Maternal Identity*. Amherst: University of Massachusetts Press, 2002.

Thurer, Shari. *Myths of Motherhood: How Culture Reinvents the Good Mother*. New York: Penguin, 1995.

van den Hengel, John. "Miriam of Nazareth: Between Symbol and History." In *A Feminist Companion to Mariology*, edited by Amy-Jill Levine and Maria Mayo Robbins, 130–46. Cleveland, Oh.: Pilgrim Press, 2005.

Vander Stichele, Caroline, and Todd C. Penner, eds. *Her Master's Tools? Feminist and Postcolonial Engagements of Historical-Critical Discourse*. Leiden: Brill, 2005.

Victor, Barbara. *Army of Roses: Inside the World of Palestinian Women Suicide Bombers*. Emmaus, PA: Rodale, 2003.

Warner, Marina. *Alone of All Her Sex: The Myth and the Cult of the Virgin Mary*. New York: Knopf, 1976.

Watson, Patricia A. *Ancient Stepmothers: Myth, Misogyny, and Reality*. Leiden: Brill Academic, 1997.

Weitzman, Steven. *Surviving Sacrilege: Cultural Persistence in Jewish Antiquity*. Cambridge, MA: Harvard University Press, 2005.

West, Traci C. *Disruptive Christian Ethics: When Racism and Women's Lives Matter*. Louisville, KY: Westminster John Knox, 2006.

Wiedemann, Thomas E. J. *Adults and Children in the Roman Empire*. New Haven, CT: Yale University Press, 1989.

Zervos, George Themelis. "Christmas with Salome." In *A Feminist Companion to Mariology*, edited by Amy-Jill Levine and Maria Mayo Robbins, 77–98. Cleveland, Oh.: Pilgrim Press, 2005.

Index of Ancient Sources

Lamentations Rabbah		20.1	89
1:16	56, 64	20.1-7	113
3	118	20.2	89, 92
Martyrdom of Marian and James		20.4	92
7.6	117	20.5	92
13.1-3	117-118	20.6	94, 96
Martyrdom of Montanus and Lucius		20.7	94
12.3	117	21.9-10	89
16.3-6	117	21.11	89
Passion of Perpetua and Felicitas			
1.1	87		
1.2	87		
1.4	86		
2.1	87, 92, 103, 113		
2.2	87, 92		
2.3	87		
3.1	103		
3.2	104		
3.2-1	87		
4	87		
4.1	92		
4.9	107		
4.10	88, 104		
5.2	87, 92		
6.2	87		
7	88		
8.1	88		
8.4	88, 108		
9.2	87		
10.7	88, 92		
10.13	92		
10.14	88, 104		
11-13	88		
14-21	88		
15	113		
15.1	88		
15.2	88, 113		
15.3	114		
15.5	114		
15.6-7	114		
16.1	114		
18.1	89		
18.2	89		
18.3	89		
18.3-4	113		

Subject Index